Mysteries
OF THE
AURA

ABOUT THE AUTHORS

Jean-Louis de Biasi is an author, lecturer, and philosopher. He is also a certified yoga teacher practicing several branches of yoga for more than forty years. He has been initiated into the highest degrees of several Western traditions, is the Grand Master of the Aurum Solis–Mediterranean Yoga, and G. P. of the Kabbalistic Order of the Rose-Cross. Prior to his involvement in American Freemasonry, he received the highest degrees in Freemasonry in Europe, including the degrees of Egyptian Freemasonry. He specializes in esoteric Freemasonry and rituals. With his wife, Patricia, he is managing the international organizations mentioned before and teaching the eight rays of Mediterranean Yoga all over the world. To learn more about Jean-Louis de Biasi, please visit him online at: www.debiasi.org.

Patricia Bourin is a certified yoga teacher with more than fifteen years of practice and a breathing coach (Pranayama). She is the Associate Grand Master of Aurum Solis–Mediterranean Yoga. Within the latter, she also teaches energy work, meditation, and visualization. In parallel of her work, she progressively became a talented mosaic artist. She is also the coauthor of *Mysteries of the Aura*. To learn more about Patricia, please visit her online at: www .bourin.us.

Mysteries
OF THE
AURA

HOW TO SEE, INTERPRET & WORK WITH SUBTLE ENERGIES

JEAN-LOUIS DE BIASI
PATRICIA BOURIN

Llewellyn Publications | Woodbury, Minnesota

FIRST EDITION
First Printing, 2023

Book design by Samantha Peterson
Cover design by Kevin R. Brown
Interior art by Mary Ann Zapalac and the Llewellyn Art Department

Llewellyn Publications is a registered trademark of Llewellyn Worldwide Ltd.

Library of Congress Cataloging-in-Publication Data (Pending)
ISBN: 978-0-7387-6381-1

Llewellyn Publications
A Division of Llewellyn Worldwide Ltd.
2143 Wooddale Drive
Woodbury, MN 55125-2989
www.llewellyn.com

Printed in the United States of America

CONTENTS

EXERCISES

DISCLAIMER

All information presented in this book is for informational purposes only. Do not rely on this information as a substitute for professional medical advice, diagnoses, or treatments. If you have any concerns or questions about your health, you should always consult with a physician or other healthcare professional. The authors of this book are not registered dietitians.

You are ultimately responsible for all decisions pertaining to your health. Each individual's dietary needs and restrictions are unique. Always consult a qualified healthcare professional before starting a new diet or health program. The authors and publisher are not responsible for adverse reactions, effects, or consequences resulting from the use of any suggestions herein.

ACKNOWLEDGMENTS

The writing of a book is often a solitary activity. However, it cannot be done without the help and support of several people.

First, I would like to thank my wife, Patricia. We have built this book together. We have discussed every chapter and practiced together the exercises offered here. I started to create and experiment with most of the techniques forty years ago. Then we taught some of these practices in workshops and in the initiatory Orders we manage. It was important to organize this material in a comprehensive way and such work has only been possible thanks to the continuous support and participation of Patricia, Associate Grand Master of the Aurum Solis.

I would like also to offer my grateful thanks to companions of the Aurum Solis who have participated in experimentations and implementations of some of these techniques.

Finally, I want to thank the team of professionals at Llewellyn Worldwide who took care of this book. Their expertise, advice, and feedback were essential and must be recognized.

FOREWORD

Magic is a verb. It isn't something that exists outside of us, like air, or something that happens to us, like fate. We make magic. We use knowledge, skill, and materials to craft our works.

Knowledge comes from people who share it and from our own experimentation. Skill comes from practice. But what are the materials that make magic happen? Musicians use strings, flutes, drums, and voices to create sounds that resonate with our hearts. Artists use colors and textures to create patterns that show us something new. We make magic with energy. Another way to put it is that we make magic with the aura.

Learning to see the aura is one of the first magical skills people develop. The aura is generally described as a halo of light surrounding the physical body. My high school friends and I would sit in a darkened room and defocus our eyes to try to glimpse the shimmering colors, then trade notes on what we saw. With more experience, we realized that the aura is a lot more than a halo. It's not a field that the physical body gives off—it's the visible overlap of the body of light with the physical body.

In the Western world, we lost the knowledge of the soul's body for some centuries. Our map of the human self has been pretty simple: body plus soul. However, looking into our past, both Pagan and Christian, we find a third element: a body in between the physical body and spirit. Today we call this the *subtle body* or the *light body*. These phrases capture the idea of energy, light, becoming physical, the body.

Spiritual systems around the world outline the physiology of the subtle body or bodies. The Hebrew Kabbalah, the wisdom of the East in Buddhist and Hindu Tantra, and the ancient Egyptians all described parts of the soul and how to work with them. The aura is the visible sign of these other bodies we inhabit. Studying the aura leads us deeper into the knowledge of ourselves as beings of light manifesting in the material world.

To work with these energies, we need a solid grounding in magical physiology and an introduction to practice. We need a guide, someone who not only understands the energies and works with them but knows how to teach them. People who share knowledge are teachers whether they are peers or have years more experience than we do. The important thing about a teacher is that they can separate their own ego from the act of teaching and focus on passing the knowledge. Jean-Louis is one of the best teachers I know.

I met Jean-Louis in a venerable mansion in St. Paul, Minnesota, at the memorial service for Carl Weschcke. A number of Llewellyn writers turned out to pay our respects to the visionary publisher. I reconnected with old friends and got to meet people I only knew from their published work.

When I was introduced to Jean-Louis, I knew him as the tenth and current Grand Master of the Aurum Solis. Now, I've spent some time with magicians in the lodge systems, and people with grand titles trend toward the autocratic, so I greeted him cautiously. He instantly put me at ease. He has the kind of quiet elegance that doesn't need to boast to impress. We spent an amiable time discussing our shared interest in the history of women's lodges in France.

Since then, I've gotten to know him better through our monthly conversations with a group of fellow magicians. Our mutual friend Hercules Invictus hosts a monthly symposium about theurgy, the ancient Greek-Egyptian magical system that underlies Western magic. From his works I knew Jean-Louis was knowledgeable. In conversation I've gotten to know him as a supportive colleague. I've seen him give confidence to a panelist who had a moment of self-doubt. He likes working with other people too; Jean-Louis is the one who is always coming up with new projects for us to do together.

Teaching subtle body physiology requires familiarity with both Eastern and Western spiritual systems. Jean-Louis combines a deep grounding in the Western mysteries with an understanding of the philosophy and practice of yoga. His breadth of knowledge is impressive, and he clearly practices what he teaches. More importantly, he encourages us all to develop our own understandings. In English, the term *mystery* carries the idea of a secret. For the ancients, the mysteries were not hidden information but, instead, initiations into a sacred experience. Jean-Louis is a modern teacher of the mysteries, inviting us in to learn for ourselves and to practice what we learn.

Mysteries of the Aura is the book I wish I'd had when I was just starting out working with the aura. It teaches how to develop the ability to perceive the shimmering colors of the light, but it goes much deeper than that. It helps us experience ourselves as beings of light in the material world. That experience is the door to creating our own magic, and this book provides the key.

Brandy Williams,
Author of *Cord Magic*

INTRODUCTION

Anyone who has been interested in the invisible world, spirituality, psychic abilities, or the occult has seen the word *aura* at some point. I first saw it on the cover of a French occult magazine when I was an adolescent. At that time, the internet didn't exist and there were only a few French books available on these topics. Some common books were writings from the Theosophical movement; the names H. P. Blavatsky, C. W. Leadbeater, and Annie Besant come to mind immediately. But the more popular books were by T. L. Rampa, a mysterious Tibetan monk, who embodied an adult-born British citizen. His famous book *The Third Eye* opened the door to this mysterious world. Back then, society had already known about black and white photos of ghosts, but a Russian couple surnamed Kirlian discovered a way to more clearly photograph what they called *the aura*, a fascinating electric light around our bodies.

It didn't take much for me to become captivated by these mysterious invisible bodies. I started to look for other books that could help me see the unseen. At the time, I didn't find anything clear or practical. I dreamt about a book that would describe, in a precise way, the nature of the aura and its role in my life. I wondered about the origin of this body of light. I tried to understand the differences between the soul, the spirit, the aura, animal magnetism, and more. Within a few months, my world—already filled with ghost stories told around fireplaces in the southwest of France—revealed a new universe. Furthermore, I had the deep feeling that it was not my first initiation to this art. Undoubtedly, I was reactivating an ability mastered in past lives.

1

A few months later, while still in high school, I created the first parapsychic organization in southwest France. I led this group to experiment and practice aura vision, hypnotism, out-of-body experiences, astral travel, and more. It was the beginning of a life dedicated to psychic and spiritual investigation, which eventually led to my initiation into the most famous Western initiatory organization.

During my younger years, I was reactivating my psychic abilities and experimenting on the public. I was organizing what became a safe and efficient method to see the subtle bodies. In the years that followed, I selected several "tricks" that allowed me to progress safely in my training while avoiding psychic obstacles and illusions. Some practical keys were still preserved in the traditional initiatory Orders that I was initiated into.

But as you'll soon understand, seeing the aura is not the only thing that matters. It is important to understand what you can see and why. Since the time I started this work, several books have been published on the topic. Sometimes these works are from an Eastern perspective, sometimes Western. The system of the chakras comes to mind immediately when I think of the East. The Western world elaborated a mix between the sefirot of Kabbalah and the Christian body of light; not many writings acknowledge this discrepancy. When we consider our physical bodies, there is no doubt about our commonalities, so why should there be any difference in our subtle bodies? If the subtle body is real, why is it different in the various systems I just mentioned? We cannot avoid these questions if we want to be honest, and this book is the right place to find answers.

I am not answering these questions from a purely theoretical standpoint. In this book, what I explain comes from direct observation over the years and from the traditions I represent. I've always thought that the ability to see the aura should be taught to anyone interested, giving you the opportunity to verify what was explained for yourself. So in this book, you will find the essential elements that can help you progress toward the vision, detection, and action of these bodies of light. The methods offered in this book have been used successfully. You should know for certain that everyone can see or detect the aura, and you can do the same. Of course, as with any art, not everyone is a virtuoso. Nevertheless, it is still possible to master the fundamentals easily and quickly.

We could stop there, after starting to see the invisible, but it is very beneficial to keep moving forward. As you'll discover, true vision of the aura is not limited to this simple ability. The desire to discover these invisible worlds is the manifestation of a deeper and more essential will. It is the reminiscence of a time when, as a spiritual being, you mastered this faculty of vision. Interest in this subject is not a coincidence. If you are reading these words, it is because an inner voice has guided you. This is a manifestation of the spiritual light starting to clear the clouds of your memory. The time has come for a deeper development of your real self.

Part One

HISTORY OF THE AURA

Chapter One
OCCULT ANATOMY

This chapter deals with occult anatomy and the nature of our subtle bodies. For now, we ask you to accept this information as working hypotheses that you can check for yourself over time. In this first description, we use the classifications and names you can find almost everywhere. Most of these classifications have been chosen by clairvoyants of the Theosophical Society, such as C. W. Leadbeater. Fascinatingly, several of their psychic observations were brought back in India and are part of the Eastern tradition. Later, the New Age movement adopted these teachings, as did the growing Buddhist and yoga traditions.

To help you easily understand the nature and role of the different subtle bodies, we begin with the material world and move progressively to the highest spiritual level. This is the easiest way to understand how the subtle bodies manifest themselves, their role, their nature, and their characteristics.

You may notice that our descriptions of auras differ in some ways from other descriptions you have seen here or there. The reason is simple: in this text we only use what we have personally verified and experienced by clairvoyance or other means. The techniques presented in this book made this research possible and enabled a presentation of the invisible world that surrounds us and remains inaccessible to most human eyes.

THE PHYSICAL BODY

For centuries, alchemists and philosophers have tried to explain the nature of the cosmos and human beings. The Hermetic principle has been summarized in the 1908 *Kybalion* with the words "As above, so below," meaning that our body is an image of the Universe. One was able to explain the other and vice versa. This is what we call the *theory of correspondences* between macrocosm (the cosmos) and microcosm (the body). For the ancient Hermetics, stars were connected to human beings, not only as a spiritual influence, but also as a physical one.

According to this traditional teaching, the physical body is formed of the classic four elements: earth, air, water, and fire, to which a fifth was added, the aether. Alchemists also identified three components of matter, which are sulfur, salt, and mercury. The four elements are not a physical reality we can directly observe and measure; elements such as water, earth, and fire are considered to be specific characters, principles, and categories that describe reality rather than analyze it. If we think about these categories from a Platonic standpoint, we would say that these elements are generic ideas located in the realm of the mind. Everything related to them is a manifestation of this unique principle. Thus, to speak of water as a principle is obviously to speak of the sea, the rivers, the rain, etc.—but it also refers to fluids in the body and in the world.

Earth is the principle of solidity and stability. Its character can be fixed in the form of stone. But earth is also manifested in sand and clay. It is this characteristic that makes us what we are, a mass of atoms that can be observed by our senses. This is the principle of materiality.

Fire is an extremely subtle element that has often been linked to light. It represents agitation, the dynamic energy that creates life. This is the medium that transmits the energy transforming and animating the world and its beings. It is the element of movement and change. The absence of fire would indicate immobility and, eventually, death. In the physical body, fire manifests itself as the energy creating and maintaining movement and life. At the same time, it is the element of consumption and must be restrained. We cannot live without this element, but it is also the cause of aging, slowing down the entire organism.

Air, also called "the divine breath" or "the sacred word," is extremely close to fire. It is considered the channel and guide of the fire element. Breath allows the air to be energized by fire. Air is the vehicle that helps us assimilate one of the subtle energies, called *prana*. To breathe is to maintain life, but also to receive the energy that makes us a living creature.

Aether, the fifth element, has no physical manifestation. It is the manifestation of the energy that holds the structure of the physical body. Aether forms the foundation of the etheric body.

For ancient alchemists and astrologers, these five principles have a psychological dimension:

- Water is the ability to adapt to circumstances and the flexibility that helps correct mistakes.

- Earth is both rigor and rigidity that can limit the ability to adapt.

- Air gives insouciance and lightness. It can inspire poets and mystics. It can also generate instability and weakness.

- Fire generates the energy we see manifested in assertive personalities. This power is reflected in their life, giving them the courage to be conquerors, innovators, and creators in the physical or spiritual worlds. In excess, fire can prevent people from seeing their mistakes.

- When aether is dominant, the individual is eager to live according to the highest moral standards, accomplishing great things for the good of their fellow human beings.

If the elements just described are well-balanced, then the body and soul can be in harmony, leading to a long and healthy life. Interactions with the world and other people should bring fulfillment and joy.

Again, such principles should not be seen as material components of matter. Modern science has proven very effective in explaining the physical world. Although some parts of these ancient teachings overlap with science, they see the world from a different perspective. Science brings rationality and efficiency. Traditional Hermetic philosophy brings symbols and meaning to the life we live. Together, they are a perfect combination for the understanding of the physical and spiritual worlds.

The physical body is the foundation of the subtle bodies. It is the repository of the soul, the Holy Grail in which the immortal part of our self lies. Every level of your being is interconnected, assembled around your inner self like onion skins around the sprout. These layers allow the communication between the highest levels of your soul and physical body. They are different levels of energy, not really material but also not totally spiritual. They can be identified as the subtle body. They maintain contact between the two worlds and with the cosmic energies. For this reason, several cultures talk about three bodies: the physical body, the intermediary, and the subtle body. I am sure you can imagine that this connection between matter and spirit cannot occur in one simple step. As the rainbow is made of multiple colors, the subtle body is made of several layers. Each one has a specific shape made of light and energy. All of them are different manifestations of what we call the *aura*.

An aura is not limited to a simple halo surrounding saints' heads. It is a generic word that is applied to these levels of vibrations. They have received various names corresponding to each step of this celestial ladder. We can talk about the etheric aura, astral aura, mental aura, and causal aura. However, you should think about them as a continuous light with gradual frequencies. The different levels of energy can be compared to different radio waves found at the same place: they all penetrate each other without breaking their own structure. It is the same for the subtle bodies around us.

The physical body has been considered by ancient Hermetists and Neoplatonists as a jail or a tomb for the soul. Depending on your past lives, the walls of this "cave" can be thicker or thinner. This difference will increase or decrease the type and amount of work you'll need to do to perceive the various levels of your aura.

But before beginning the first exercise, we must realize that the physical body should be as balanced as possible. This process brings you health and can facilitate your current training. The communication taking place between the environment and the body has evolved over time. Indeed, when we live, breathe, and eat, we assimilate nutrients and pure energy that sustain our physical life. This subtle energy you are about to perceive is part of your auras and brings them life and health. This is why diet is important.

In the seventies, I was following an intense training to see the auras. As I was working on the etheric level, I had a surprising experience. One day I attended a lecture on art and archaeology. The speaker was talking in front of a blackboard. The light was coming from the side, which is the best way to exercise this specific vision. After a few minutes, I started to observe his etheric aura. The usual color of the etheric aura is light blue, very close to the smoke of incense. After a few seconds of gazing, a golden color started to appear. Soon the whole aura was light gold and white, with only some areas remaining blue. It was a real surprise, and I started to doubt my perception. Perhaps fatigue was twisting my vision? Then the lecturer revealed that he was following a specific diet and was vegetarian. This was a revelatory explanation for me. Other examinations of the same kind over the years have confirmed a real interaction between diet and individual energy.

To a certain extent, the health of our psychic bodies is linked to our physical bodies and our diet. Moreover, our ability to progress spiritually is in large part related to the attitude developed toward our physical envelope.

For centuries, vegetarianism has been considered one of the best solutions for purifying the body. This is not the place to discuss the merits of this diet. However, we should understand the link between the food we absorb and its specific energy, which is eventually assimilated by the aura. Eating animals does not have the same impact on the spiritual bodies as eating plants. The physical assimilation is different, and the subtle assimilation is just as delicate. After being vegetarian for more than ten years when I was young, I eventually stopped. Today, my wife Patricia and I practice and teach the Mediterranean diet.[1] Meat is allowed, though it is recommended to eat a small quantity. You see, it is not the meat itself that is a problem, but its origin—the way it is processed and consumed.

To simplify, we can say that some animals have a high consciousness, close to that of humans. This consciousness creates a chain reaction on the physical and invisible level. When animals are slaughtered violently, a physical reaction occurs in the meat. There is another effect on the invisible level: the violence of the slaughter combined with the fear felt by the animal rejects

1. The Mediterranean diet is the only diet recommended by the American Heart Association. In brief, this diet includes plenty of fruits, vegetables, grains, potatoes, beans, nuts, and seeds. Olive oil is a primary fat source. Dairy products, eggs, fish, and meat are consumed in low to moderate amounts. Jean-Louis de Biasi has a certificate in Mediterranean Food and Diet from the University of Athens.

the astral bodies that create an agglomerate of energy. This bad energy, full of fear and stress, becomes almost an autonomous entity and remains attached to the meat as an anchor. On the physical level, this kind of meat can be very difficult to assimilate. On the invisible level, the remaining traumatized consciousness is seeking a host that can guarantee its survival. Our aura can then be parasitized by something like a "ghost," a consciousness using our personal energy for its own sake. The consciousness of plants is lower; although they have reactions, they are easier to manage.

Therefore, should we conclude that we must all become vegetarians? Actually, the answer is no. Being vegetarian for a certain period of time can help purify your physical body and aura. If you do not continue the diet indefinitely, you'll still be able to repeat the experience over shorter periods of time to pursue specific trainings. It is beneficial to find a balance; avoid any extreme. Being able to adapt our diet to the various contexts of our life, avoiding excess and always choosing organic food humanely raised and killed, should be the way to go.

There are traditional ways to approach the animal and communicate using words, prayers, and invocations. The goal here is to speak to the spirit of the animal and explain that you need its life to survive in good health. An invocation should be used to invite the animal's soul to join another plane and continue its development. This attitude is often associated with a fast and painless slaughtering. Sometimes most of the blood is removed, which is the main vehicle of vital energy. In modern society, such ritual is not often practiced. Consequently—and even if you know the animal has been humanely raised—it is important to fulfill the role of the priest and to declaim a short prayer before any preparation or ingestion of meat. Address the spirit of the animal, helping any remaining parts of its soul move on. We can assure you that doing this has the potential to change many things in your body and your aura.

What we just explained regarding meat can apply to other kinds of food as well, and for great benefit. You can also continue this exploration by thinking about everything you absorb, from beverages to music, television, social media, etc. Avoid excess and anything that creates addiction.

So far, we have focused on the physical body because this first body supports the others; it is the center around which subtle bodies are organized. It also plays an important role in channeling the energies received by all levels of your aura. If the physical body is cared for, these energies will flow freely and more efficiently.

THE ETHERIC BODY

One important and fascinating topic is the limit and dimension of the aura. This topic is not a simple curiosity. It helps to explain several kinds of phenomena linked to our subtle bodies that occur away from our physical body.

The aura and the aether, also called *prana*, have strong similarities. The energy circulating in the etheric body is mainly coming from this cosmic energy. If you want to imagine what auras look like, imagine dropping a small amount of paint on a wet sheet of paper. The color of the drop's center is denser, and thin filaments radiate from it. Now imagine you do the same with several drops of different colors in the same place so that the colors blend or keep their own nature. This is what auras can look like. The main difference is that the aura's color do not mix, as they belong to different vibratory planes.

In the paint example, colors have a limit, but the waves of energy that comprise the auras do not—they extend to the infinite. Think of the concentric waves created on the surface of a lake after throwing in a rock. This analogy allows you to understand that the rock creates a chain reaction that affects the entire lake. If you replace the water with aether, then you have the image of the aura, both visible and infinite. In the cosmos, the auras of all living beings interpenetrate, sometimes harmoniously, sometimes not. But the vibration of a particular frequency created by the aura stays connected with us no matter the distance. Quantum physics explains how two things can react in synchrony even if they are apparently separated, which also explains why an action from distance is possible. But even if we have the potential to achieve this spiritual work, it requires a real training and control of our abilities.

———

The first of the subtle bodies is called the *etheric*. In this book we use the terms *etheric*, *etheric body*, and *etheric aura* interchangeably. The etheric is a level of energy so close to the physical plane that it almost belongs to it, but this body is the first aura that is not immediately visible to the naked eye. The etheric is the occult energetic structure of your body; think of it as a duplication of yourself made of vital energy.

Being a luminous counterpart of the physical body, the etheric is intertwined with it. It is not an independent subtle body, although in some conditions it can be partially detached (see chapter 13). The etheric penetrates your whole body, which is literally immersed in these waves of energy. It constitutes your body's energy foundation.

To illustrate this, imagine a magnetic piece of metal. When you look at it with the naked eye, you do not see anything besides its material appearance. But if you hold a sheet of paper above it and sprinkle some iron filings on the paper, the magnetic field is "magically" revealed. The planet also generates a powerful magnetic field, and we can imagine a similar etheric around it. These magnetic fields are present but difficult to observe. The etheric vibrates at a higher level than magnetism; that makes it almost undetected. However, Kirlian photography revealed a manifestation of this energy for the first time.

It is difficult to see the etheric within the body. However, this energy extends above the surface of the skin by a few inches. Consequently, the etheric is easier to observe in this zone as the physical body does not block view of it.

Description

The etheric is a luminous body that looks like the shining smoke of incense. Its color may vary, but it is usually a very light blue that radiates from the surface of the skin. The densest part constitutes the occult structure of the physical body and is not strictly limited to the surface of the skin. The radiance of this body is usually one-half inch (one centimeter) above the skin. About one inch (two and a half centimeters) from the skin, the etheric is less dense and can be seen as very thin rays of light that gradually fade away from the body.

Within the physical body, the etheric is usually deep blue, close to ultramarine. The colors of the filaments or rays change substantially as they extend from the denser center. For example, they may become a deeper blue, light purple, or golden. It should be noted that in some cases, the color of the etheric may vary considerably. The vegetarian speaker discussed earlier had a mostly golden etheric.

The etheric is covered by channels of energy, sometimes very thin, that are reminiscent of the brain's neuron structure. These bright connections, called *nadis*, are used in energy work. They converge on several centers located in precise parts of the body. Some of these webs of energy are called *chakras* in the Eastern tradition, which means "wheels" in Sanskrit.

Function

The function of the etheric body is to ensure the cohesion and circulation of energy within the physical body. For this reason, the etheric body attracts the energy from what we called the *aether*, and more precisely, what is called *prana* in the Eastern tradition. It also ensures circulation and balances vital energy.

There are particles of energy present all around us and in every living being. They manifest in the form of small, transparent spheres. (They are usually one-eighth in diameter, or a few millimeters.) Their color is difficult to describe. Often, we perceive their brightness but cannot discern a particular color. In their natural state, the energy particles are agitated by a frenetic dance, an incessant agitation that nevertheless does not alter their location.

Our physical bodies assimilate these energy particles in two ways. We absorb them through our breathing and everything that occurs in the respiratory process. In addition, they are attracted by our chakras.

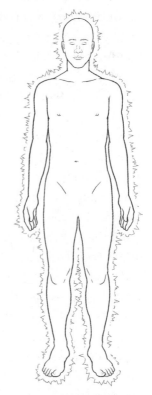

The Etheric Body

In the case of animals and plants, the circulation of energy occurs according to patterns specific to each one. We should note that the appearance of the etheric in animals and plants is significantly different from ours, since it may sometimes consist of brighter colors that tend toward gold and white.

Outdoor locations have their own level of energy. With time, you can see and use this energy, which can be restorative or destructive. The earth, as previously stated, has an energetic field that is structured according to ley lines and the world's telluric current, revealed by the German physician Ernst Hartmann. It is possible to detect these webs using radiesthesia. This study of energy is called *geobiology*. We will talk more about this in chapter 10.

In mindfulness workshops, we use the connection between the energy in the ground and the astral vision. My wife, Patricia, and I have conducted several workshops in the past, and I can recall how students reacted when we helped them find this inner perception. One experience took place in the south of France, in an ancient sacred space that was used by Cro-Magnons forty thousand years ago. The presence of painted caves nearby was one of their visible traces. Two of the students were having a difficult time disconnecting from the visible world. We were in a meadow close to a beautiful cliff in the middle of a forest. I asked them to walk barefoot and to wear a blindfold. I then guided them in a silent and slow walk, asking them to relax, breathe, and focus on the sensations of their feet on the grass and the air on their skin. I invited them to welcome any difference of sensation on their physical body. Walking in silence side by side, they noticed variations of temperature under their feet and a rise of vibrations on their faces at very specific locations. The reactions of both students were very similar: sometimes the general feeling was appeasing, and sometimes it was very tense and unpleasant. This kind of practice is a great way to open the door to our inner abilities.

As stated earlier, the etheric vanishes a few inches above the skin. This is not because it ends there, but because the density of the remaining subtle body makes it difficult to see. Because of this difference of density, seeing the next body, the astral aura, can be tricky.

The Nadis

We have already mentioned the channels of life energy (prana) called *nadis*. This word comes from the Sanskrit root *nada*, which means "to flow." Nadis can be compared to tubes of different sizes, through which energy flows. It is said that there are seventy-two thousand nadis in our energy body.

There is a strange similarity between the nervous system and the nadis. A representation of the nadis placed beside the nervous system shows a fascinating web made of thousands of connections between larger or thinner channels of light. Fourteen nadis are larger and more important than the others. Among the fourteen, three can be considered major.

The main pathway following the vertical axis of the spine is called the *sushumna nadi* and connects the bottom of the vertebral column to the pineal gland. The ida nadi connects the same two centers and is intertwined with the sushumna nadi, going from the left nostril down the spine. Pingala nadi intertwines in the same way and goes from the right nostril down the spine, symmetrical to the ida nadi. Both spiral around the center axis and cross each other on the chakras. By their energetic interlacing, these three nadis create the symbol well-known in the Western world as the caduceus.

Prana is manifested in the body in the form of these two currents and must be balanced. The currents are associated with the solar force (pingala) and the lunar force (ida). Lama Anagarika Govinda states, "Solar energies represent diurnal forces, that is, centrifugal forces tending to certainty, knowledge, discrimination, and thus to differentiation and intellect. Lunar energies symbolize nocturnal forces, centripetal forces exercised in the darkness of the unconscious, undifferentiated, regenerative flows from the eternal source of life tend to reunify."[2]

Sushumna is the axis of the world and the link between the seven main energy centers. It is, at the same time, a balance and harmonization of these two types of energies, lunar and solar, immaterial and material. It is the symbol of latent potentialities that, for some, slumber at the bottom of the spine in the symbolic shape of a snake called Kundalini. The examination of movements in these nadis can be valuable in detecting the distribution of energy and any problems related to it. Let us summarize the characteristics of these two nadis:

Ida Nadi: Moon, left nostril, cold, female, mental, parasympathetic, blue

Pingala Nadi: Sun, right nostril, hot, male, physical, sympathetic, red

The Chakras

Etymologically, the word *chakras* refers to wheels, and they appear similar if you observe these centers of energy. This book is not an exhaustive work

---

2. Govinda, *Foundations of Tibetan Mysticism*.

about chakras, but we are going to provide a summary of what you should know about them. It is important to understand the chakras' roles and to be able to directly observe them. Observation is the best way to understand how many there are, their location, and their importance.

Among other things, chakras receive several levels of energy, including prana. But each one also emits an energy with a specific frequency. Consequently, someone whose inner development is centered on the astral plane would radiate from the solar plexus and influence their environment on the same plane. It is the same for all the other centers. Chakras appear as swirls of light along the spine and perpendicular to it. Seen from the front of the body, they look like very bright wheels of light. The energy is sucked up, circulates in the nadis and the body, and then is rejected. The flow rejected by the chakras is constant, but this is not true of the power entering these centers. The light is very dense when approaching these centers; energy can enter from the side, the front, and sometimes even the back. Although it's not an absolute rule, most people attract energy from the sides of the chakras.

The number of chakras has never been definitive and can vary considerably. Sometimes, some chakras with similar functions or body locations are merged. Several chakra systems exist in the Eastern world. The most common systems include six major chakras, twenty-two minor, and eighty-six secondary chakras, for a total of 114. Among the minor, some are still essential, such as the chakra of the heart (hrit chakra).[3] Consequently, the number, importance, and attributions are more a question for philosophical schools rather than the result of direct exploration.

In this book, we use a system of seven chakras, six in the body and the seventh above the head. C. W. Leadbeater came to this conclusion after carefully observing the occult structure of several subjects working with him. Our own research has confirmed this number, regardless of cultural or religious background.

When you attempt to observe the chakras, it is best to start by standing on the side of the subject. After this first vision, you should move to the front to

---

3. Hrit chakra is different than the anahata chakra, commonly known as the heart chakra. Hrit (or *Hridaya*, "heart") is below anahata. Hrit is the secret heart chakra. It is sometimes called the surya (sun) chakra. It is symbolized by a double square and a tree and has eight petals.

observe the very inner part of the chakra. This cone of light rotates around its center. The light that emits is not very visible when it first leaves the chakra but becomes clearly visible a few inches from it. On the other hand, the currents of light that penetrate the chakra are clearly visible in the heart of the vortex.

This section provides the locations, colors, and symbols associated with each chakra. However, you may notice that their positions or colors may change due to various factors. All of this should be recorded during your observation so you can compare the different cases and reach your own personal conclusions.

Several symbols have been used to represent chakras. Two are extremely common. Flowers, mainly lotus, with a specific number of petals are often combined with the second representation, geometric patterns. Lotus flowers are powerful symbols found in India and Egypt. They are often linked to a world creation story. Geometrical representations are closer to an archetypal symbol of the centers and closely related to the mental and causal planes.

Let us now summarize the chakra system to give you the elements you should keep in mind when exploring the subtle bodies of a subject. From the bottom of the spine to the top of the head, the seven chakras are:

1. Muladhara chakra (root chakra)
2. Svadhishthana chakra (sacral chakra)
3. Manipura chakra (solar plexus chakra)
4. Anahata chakra (heart chakra)
5. Vishuddha chakra (throat chakra)
6. Ajna chakra (third eye chakra)
7. Sahasrara chakra (crown chakra)

Muladhara Chakra

Also Called: Root chakra

Organ(s): Perineum

Corresponding Physical Location: External organs of reproduction/ sexual organs

Approximate Position: Fourth sacral vertebra, base of the spine

Sympathetic Plexus: Coccygeal plexus

Element: Earth

Positive Effects: Health, dialectics, knowledge

Negative Effects: Obtuse materialism, conservatism

Symbolic Color: Yellow

Symbolic Form: Square

Number of Petals: Four

Mantra (Eastern Tradition): Lam

Vowel (Western Tradition): A, the Greek letter alpha, pronounced as "a" in *father*; D

This is the root chakra. It corresponds to the base of the spine. It is symbolized by a flower of four scarlet petals surrounding a yellow square with an elephant. It represents the element earth. In the center of this square, the red downward-pointing triangle represents the female genitals, in the center of which is the dark blue phallus of Shiva. A serpent, the symbol of Kundalini, is wrapped around this phallus. This is a symbol only, and these representations are not actually visible in the aura. However, the symbol gives us precious indications of the energies involved in this chakra, which must gradually be mastered to awaken one's spiritual being. Remember that such symbols can be used in meditation, creative visualization, and yoga nidra to work with the chakra. This is true for each chakra.

The awakening of this chakra confers a magnificent health, a mastery of speech, and access to a superior knowledge of the Universe. But all energy centers can develop opposite trends in the case of bad behavior or absence of morals. These trends can also be a side effect of a blocked chakra or a chakra with a reduced activity. The negative aspects of the root chakra are excessive attachment to the physical world, obtuse materialism, and selfish conservatism.

Svadhishthana Chakra

Also Called: Sacral chakra

Organ(s): Sexual organs

Corresponding Physical Location: Inner organs of elimination and reproduction

Approximate Position: First lumbar vertebra, spleen

Sympathetic Plexus: Splenic plexus

Element: Water

Positive Effects: Dissipation of ignorance, literary and poetic creativity, eloquence

Negative Effects: Low sensuality, lassitude, disgust, laziness, cruelty

Symbolic Color: White

Symbolic Form: Crescent moon

Number of Petals: Six

Mantra (Eastern Tradition): Vam

Vowel (Western Tradition): E, the Greek letter epsilon, pronounced as "e" in *set*; E flat

The sacral chakra corresponds to the sexual organs, although it is not always clearly located. It is associated with the water element. It is the reservoir of subconscious memories belonging to past lives. Its symbol is a vermillion, six-petalled flower that contains the eight-petalled white lotus, symbol of water. In the center is a crescent moon and the symbolic representation of the god of the waters. The sacral chakra is associated with language and the hands.

The awakening of this chakra confers the dissipation of ignorance, the mastery of yoga, literary and poetic creativity, eloquence, and the irresistible power of attraction. Improper functioning of this chakra may create low sensuality, lassitude, disgust, shame, laziness, contempt, suspicion, or cruelty.

Manipura Chakra

Also Called: Solar plexus chakra

Organ(s): Lumbar region

Corresponding Physical Location: Nutrition system

Approximate Position: Eighth thoracic vertebra, navel

Sympathetic Plexus: Celiac plexus

Element: Fire

Positive Effects: Balance and humility

Negative Effects: Pride, jealousy, hatred

Symbolic Color: Red

Symbolic Form: Triangle

Number of Petals: Ten

Mantra (Eastern Tradition): Ram

Vowel (Western Tradition): Θ, the Greek letter theta, pronounced as "a" in *care*; F

This chakra corresponds to the height of the navel. It is associated with the element of fire. It is the force of development of the Universe, origin of the vital fire. It is symbolically represented by ten black-gray petals framing a red triangle pointing down. A ram is presented. It is associated with the eyes and the anus.

The awakening of this chakra confers a perfect balance and the development of great humility. Improper functioning may create pride, jealousy, betrayal, hatred, or worldliness.

Anahata Chakra

Also Called: Heart chakra

Organ(s): Heart

Corresponding Physical Location: Vascular system

Approximate Position: Heart

Sympathetic Plexus: Cardiac plexus

Element: Air

Positive Effects: Intellectual intuition, prosperity, happiness, compassion, asceticism

Negative Effects: Anxiety, indecision, regret, selfishness

Symbolic Color: Blue-gray

Symbolic Form: Hexagram

Number of Petals: Twelve

Mantra (Eastern Tradition): Yam

Vowel (Western Tradition): I, Greek letter iota, pronounced as "e" in *meet*; G

This chakra is linked to the heart. It refers to the air element. It is associated with delicacy, emotional intelligence, and intellectual intuition. We must not think of it as a pure disembodied mysticism because it holds a detachment linked to the intelligence that participates to the air element. The heart chakra's symbol has twelve vermillion-red petals framing the six-pointed star composed of two intertwined triangles, representing air. Inside is an antelope. This central character makes it the center of the exchange of the vital and spiritual energies corresponding analogically to the lower and higher centers of being. It is the meeting of earth and heaven. It is here that the balance of being is constituted and that the great struggle is played out to define the way a being truly embodies their spiritual path. To live your quest in your mind is one thing, but to embody it is often another.

The awakening of this chakra leads to mastery of poetic creation, prosperity, success, happiness in this world, compassion, and the practice of asceticism. Improper functioning may create anxiety, indecision, regret, excess attachment, or subtle selfishness.

Vishuddha Chakra

Also Called: Throat chakra

Organ(s): Throat, cervical region

Corresponding Physical Location: Respiratory system

Approximate Position: Third cervical vertebra, throat

Sympathetic Plexus: Pharyngeal plexus

Element: Aether

Positive Effects: Eloquence, detachment, peace of mind, longevity

Negative Effects: Difficulty of speech

Symbolic Color: White

Symbolic Form: Triangle, tip down

Number of Petals: Sixteen

Mantra (Eastern Tradition): Ham

Vowel (Western Tradition): O, Greek letter omicron, pronounced as "o" in *hot*; A flat

This chakra is located in the throat and cervical region. Its element is aether. Symbolically, it has sixteen dark purple petals framing the representation of a white sky, in the middle of which is the triangle of the Goddess, tip turned down. In the center is another circle. The animal is the elephant.

The throat chakra corresponds to the faculty of speech, the mouth, hearing, and the ears. It confers the detachment and appeasement of the spirit. It makes avoidance of diseases and pain possible and is associated with longevity.

Ajna Chakra

Also Called: Third eye chakra

Organ(s): Frontal lobe

Corresponding Physical Location: Reflex nervous system

Approximate Position: Forehead

Sympathetic Plexus: Carotid plexus

Positive Effects: Vision free of illusions

Negative Effects: Lack of concentration, delusion

Symbolic Color: Indigo

Symbolic Form: Triangle, tip down

Number of Petals: Two

Mantra (Eastern Tradition): Aum

Vowel (Western Tradition): Y, Greek letter upsilon, pronounced as "u" in *blue*; B

This chakra corresponds to the fontanel and the mind. It receives information and redistributes it to the sensory organs. This center constitutes a boundary between the pure and abstract principles, which are above, and the denser ones that are below. Its symbolic representation has two petals that frame a white circle in which is the female triangle, pointing down. Black antelopes are associated with this chakra in ancient Hindu teachings.

The opening and mastery of this center allows us to first perceive the aura and the occult structure of our being. In a more advanced way, the awakening of the chakra allows us to pass from a partial vision of the world to a clear understanding of what illusions are. Whoever reaches this level will find it impossible to return to the deceptive nature of the physical world.

Sahasrara Chakra

Also Called: Crown chakra

Organ(s): Parietal lobe of the brain

Corresponding Physical Location: Brain (pineal gland)

Approximate Position: Top of or above the head

Sympathetic Plexus: Central nervous system

Positive Effects: Freedom, illumination

Negative Effects: Delusion, frustration, destructive urges, depression

Symbolic Color: Bright white

Symbolic Form: Large open flower

Number of Petals: One thousand

Mantra (Eastern Tradition): Om

Vowel (Western Tradition): Ω, Greek letter omega, pronounced as "o" in *only*; C

This chakra is not always considered as a center in itself by Eastern texts. Indeed, it is beyond all manifestation, and its perception cannot reflect its reality. However, the energy it releases is often seen as an intense and subtle flow above the occiput. It is very difficult to physically locate this center, as it has a much higher level of vibration than the body. The symbol is a thousand-petalled white chakra striped by energy beams of red light. The mastery and openness of this chakra obviously expresses illumination, the eternal detachment from the physical world, and the breaking of the wheel of rebirths.

There is a close relationship between this chakra and the energy center of the heart. This link helps us avoid disconnection with the world and our fellow human beings. Empathy results from it.

THE ASTRAL AURA

The astral aura is the first of the subtle bodies that, though centered on our physical envelope, considerably exceeds its dimension and vibration. This is usually what is known as *aura*. Before going into specifics, it may be useful to explain the aura's role and function.

This aura is the manifestation of our emotions and memories. It can be thought of as the subtle image of our temperament. Our feelings can interact with it, changing secondary colors temporarily. The astral aura is, above all, the reflection of your being as it really is, even if you are not aware of it. It reveals our true nature beyond the psychological and social masks that our knowledge creates. As you can imagine, seeing another person's aura is an access to real intimacy. Consequently, we must keep these observations confidential—it is a huge responsibility that we must honor with integrity.

The astral aura can indicate psychological and physical issues. The past has also created marks in our aura that can influence much of our character and many of our behaviors. It is a living memory that belongs to each of us, but it is also the result of our education, environment, and interactions with others.

Description

The astral aura has an ovoid shape, the base of which is usually between two and four inches (five and ten centimeters) under the feet and between eight and twelve inches (twenty and thirty centimeters) above the head. At the height of your chest, it has a radius between two and three feet (sixty centimeters to one meter). These dimensions are averages resulting from different observations Patricia and I have done during our hundreds of aura readings. Auric dimensions can vary significantly from one individual to another depending on the stage of psychic training and karma.

The shape and dimensions we just indicated do not mean that this body has the same appearance as the physical or etheric bodies. Two different things should be distinguished here: the astral body itself, and the astral aura, which is closely linked to the physical body. The astral aura is what we have just described. With that being said, trying to describe the aura is like trying to describe another world to one who has never seen it, or trying to describe a master's painting to an individual blind from birth.

The astral aura consists of ribbons of light rippling around the body, with an appearance similar to aurora borealis. The light is a shimmering stream rolling around the body. It is a luminous presence that has a dominant color and secondary colors. It has an elusive and changing nature, which makes it mysterious and fascinating. These ribbons of light sometimes move in connection with the chakras, as the ribbons are their distant and more subtle emanations.

The aura's specific character is made from these various colored layers. Some of them constitute the background and are considered the foundation of this plane; they are the result of character, experience, and personality. These colors can change, but they do so more slowly than the other layers. Auric colors can connect with other waves of light as delicate shades. If you have ever observed drops of ink dripping in a glass of water, this is similar to movement that can occur in the aura. In the astral aura, colors are much lighter and more evanescent than ink.

The movement of these currents of light can be fast or slow. If you consider being at the center of a circle, they usually rotate clockwise around your body. These ribbons of light typically move horizontally but can also circulate at different angles. Each case is different and has a specific meaning. In some areas, the colors are more diffuse or even nonexistent. In others, they are highly concentrated. This repartition of light is not random and has a direct relation with us as organisms. Some modifications may start at this level and have later repercussions on the etheric and physical level.

During an aura reading, it is necessary to learn how to distinguish what belongs strictly to the aura without any connection to the physical body and what is likely to have a direct link to it. Usually what is related to the body is closer to it; this may give the impression that the colors are trying to stick to the body and create marks on it. They are less luminous than the rest of this subtle body. It is important to evaluate the density of the color, light or opaque.

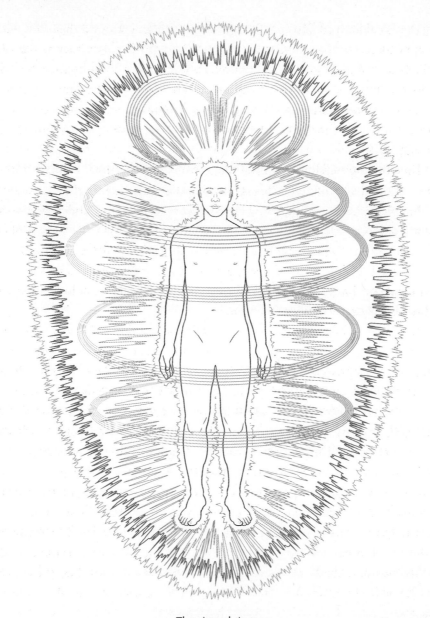

The Astral Aura

Other modifications of color, on the other hand, are intimately linked to emotions. They are the result of urges, and although they usually have a limited duration, they create a sudden change in the aura. For example, it is possible to see bright red "lightning bolts" when someone is violently irritated.

A greenish ribbon of light appearing in front of the body is a sign of a lie. I must admit, I used this observation often when my daughters were young. At the time, I was exploring all the aspects of the aura. I loved looking at their auras when they were playing and soon began to observe a very characteristic color when they were not telling the truth about something. It didn't take long for them to notice that I was looking at their auras while asking questions about specific situations. After explaining what I was doing and seeing, lies became impossible. Even still today, they know that such manifestations are real, and they remember this change in their lives.

A color that spreads all around manifests a state of meditation. When these luminous currents become foggy and slow down, it indicates that the subject is intoxicated with alcohol or drugs. If this habit is occasional, it doesn't affect the deepest parts of the astral aura, but long-term behaviors can have lasting changes, whether positive (meditation, spiritual elevation, etc.) or negative (drugs, tobacco, alcohol, etc.).

Function

The aura is the emotional memory of what we live and feel. Living in an unhealthy atmosphere and/or being in contact with individuals who cultivate morbid tendencies can gradually contaminate our astral aura. It will eventually lead us to a similar state of consciousness. We can even feel the effects several months after the situation has improved. For example, a consequence might be that we feel extremely strong desires for no apparent reason. Consequently, our characters can change and we can feel a strange need to have experiences we wouldn't otherwise crave. This can be explained by an impregnation of our aura in the previous months or years. This magnetic presence will try to survive and increase by pushing us to give it more energy. Of course, the same thing can happen in a positive way. Thus, a good education highlighting art, literature, and philosophy can point a child in the right direction for life. Let's not forget that emotions and passions are the result of this astral body. Cultivating noble and elevated intentions strongly contributes to our development and spiritualization. More importantly, in this way, we can have a very positive influence on others.

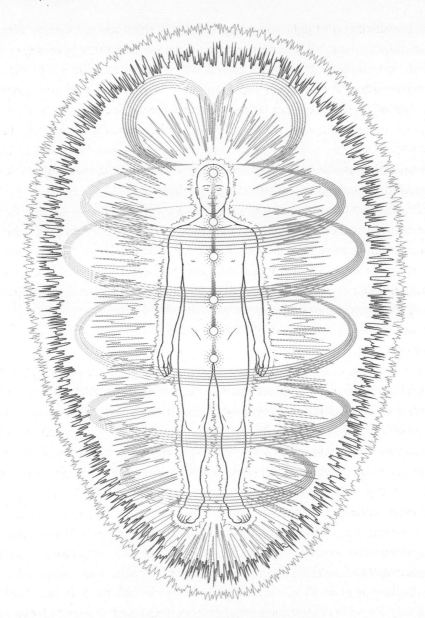

The Astral Aura and the Auric Sheath

The ribbons of light turn around the body as if it is a magnetic pole. Beyond its periphery is a very thin shell that includes the totality of the astral aura. We call this shell the *auric sheath* or *auric envelope*. Imagine an empty space without color. Nothing seems to flow in this zone. Outside it is something like a dense membrane, usually a dark beige color. It is transparent, not always easy to see. This thin layer isolates and filters external influences. In addition, this sheath acts as a screen on which can be projected very old images belonging to our karmic memory. It could be memories from this life or episodes belonging to past lives. These scenes appear as short films that come alive as soon as our consciousness focuses on them. They can be used as doors to an even deeper analysis of our self.

THE MENTAL AURA

With the mental aura, we enter a dimension even subtler than the previous ones. It is the first "body" that constitutes a recording of past lives. Its shape is different from the physical body and usually looks like an egg on its base or inverted. The size of this body is extremely variable because it depends on two factors: the karmic heritage (which, as its name suggests, contains experience gained in past lives) and the work done during this incarnation.

Description

The mental body is centered on the chest. Its size can vary from a diameter of eleven inches (thirty centimeters) to more than three feet (one meter). This body can exceed the size of the physical body. Its colors can be as variable as those of the aura, but their interpretations are different. In an aura reading of the mental body, it is more important to focus on brightness and clarity than the colors themselves. As a matter of fact, some auras are very dim while others are extremely luminous.

Much like the astral aura, the mental aura has a thin sheath. This doesn't mean that this aura is separated from everything else, but it is delimited by this envelope.

Function

As its name suggests, the mental aura is directly related to our mental activities, but we must be careful to not reduce it to the activity of our mind. The human definition of intelligence does not exactly correspond to the realities we can observe on the mental plane. As Annie Besant rightly points out, its role is twofold: on one hand, it is the vehicle of our consciousness in the mental plane. On the other hand, it enables us to act on envelopes that are inferior in density and manifest our intelligence.[4] Given the links between memory and the development of the self, this body grows as moral values are cultivated. Therefore, we can clearly distinguish someone who has cultivated the highest level of consciousness from someone who is not interested in such inner work. The mental aura of an individual who practices some sort of spiritual exercise can be very different from their physical body, which can show signs of aging. If we work spiritually and develop our psychic abilities, then the mental aura strengthens and increases in brightness. It will gradually look like a delicate weave of light radiating all around us.

Moreover, we can say that the mental aura is the center of the ego. It is necessary here to really understand what this concept means. The ego is the inner part of us expressed by the word *I*. It is this part that differentiates us from others, by affirming who we are and what belongs to us. When we talk about our self, the ego, our consciousness, we are referring to something immaterial and unimaginable. On the other hand, auric training helps us cross the threshold of the subtle planes and approach another reality.

The constitution of this body and aura are interesting. At the dawn of humanity, almost nothing differentiated humans from animals. Then, an advanced primate began to change and evolve. His brain increased and the shape of his skull changed. Consciousness progressively emerged as he started to consider himself as independent from the group he belonged to. Until this time, tribal consciousness was strong and the individual as such did not exist. The disappearance of a member of the tribe was not tragic, as the survival of the group was the most important consideration. But evolution accelerated this process, increasing this individual consciousness and allowing us to use the "I" to distinguish ourselves from the environment and the group. This is the moment when the embryo of the mental body appeared. The idea of independence grew, giving birth to new abilities such as the development of new ideas, inventions, etc. Furthermore, the mental body does not disappear after we die. What we study—the affirmation of our individual and essential identities—is the process of developing this body and planning our future lives.

4. Besant, *Man and His Bodies.*

There are two opposing attitudes that can occur coming from a previous existence:

1. In the first case, we surrender to a conformism that erases in us all individualism and original thought. We follow dominant ideologies. Critical thinking does not exist and we do not seek to exercise our intelligence. Not training our mental faculties, we absorb the ideas and influences of others.

2. In the second case, on the contrary, we seek to cultivate ourselves and develop this inner richness that gives us the capacity for free thinking. Any study, any reading will therefore aim at our development and the affirmation of a fully conscious self.

Of course, the mental body and its aura are different. In the first case, this subtle body is small and appears in a dull way. For some individuals, it can simply disappear. The boundaries of this aura are very weak, almost invisible. Such an individual is no longer critical and lucid. They will have a life very similar to that of an animal. In the second case, the mental aura is luminous, clear, and moving harmoniously.

It is important to say a few words about how to maintain and develop this body. When the soul descends into the physical body, it brings with it a karmic heritage that is different for each of us. It is something very difficult to observe directly without advanced training. At this stage of development, the shape, size, and color are a consequence of memory coming from a previous life. Then, the embodiment in physical form will progressively change

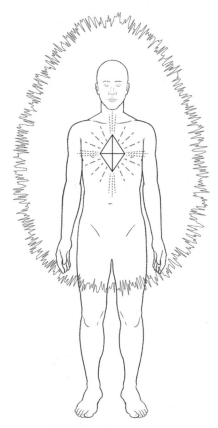

The Mental Aura
and Causal Body

the nature of this mental body. It will evolve as everything learned and done is incorporated.

We can use the analogy of the physical brain of a child. The characteristics of this organ are almost the same, regardless of the child, although there are some hereditary differences. Environmental stimuli will help create the brain connections, gradually reaching a complexity we can observe. If, during this period, the child was placed in complete darkness without contact, their brain would not develop, and this process would be irreversible. The mental body works in a similar way. We should give the child various ways to improve this subtle body. Improvement can be achieved in various ways, all aiming toward developing concentration, thinking, curiosity, etc. Everything should contribute to develop the child's consciousness. This kind of mental education at a young age allows the development of a strong mental body, constantly growing brighter, that can be easily developed through adulthood. Unfortunately, most of Western society does not prioritize critical thinking and the exercise of concentration—quite the opposite, in fact. These faculties need to be developed in order to express the best a human being can offer.

We must also learn to distinguish the ideas that belong to us from those that don't. We must regularly make an effort to observe our thoughts and strongly scrutinize others before making decisions. As for the thoughts we accept, it is necessary to cultivate them with passion. However, the goal is not to become egocentric and intolerant of other opinions. The goal is to become who we are, and this task starts with a confrontation of the identity we have developed from our experiences and the world around us.

These considerations are essential, as everything has a counterpart on the spiritual plane. Consequently, our ideas and behaviors affect the mental body and can be seen by those who have been properly trained. Two different kinds of manifestation can be observed:

1. Thoughts or mental representations are visible in an abstract form. They may appear as colored spheres (purple, blue, green, etc.) that flow near the head and follow various trajectories before vanishing. Other shapes can be generated by the activation of the mind. We are usually unaware of this phenomenon.

2. It is also possible to see more precise images, either on the membrane that delimits the mental body or in the luminous substance itself.

Of note is a strange phenomenon that can occur in the first case. When the spheres of color are dense enough, it is possible for the observer to focus on them. Then, these spheres will manifest images in the form of representations or small emanations of the unconscious.

These mental images are very important. They run through the mental body, but also influence the other subtle bodies and the physical body itself. This is the foundation of the popular method of self-improvement founded in the nineteenth century by a French pharmacist and psychologist named Émile Coué. By repeating a word or sentence, we influence the deepest levels of our unconscious, eventually changing our daily life. We have the example of the famous phrase "Every day, in every way, I'm getting better and better." This positive affirmation affects the mental body, generating new agglomerates that can influence all the levels of our being. The same thing occurs with destructive thoughts, which can invade our psyche. The state of depression is a good example for that. It is very difficult to treat this kind of problem, as it originates in the mental body and becomes, in a sense, an autonomous mental creature living at your expense. The importance of selecting thoughts that can positively influence or protect us should be clear by now.

Finally, there is a structure that belongs to the causal body but can be detected and used at the mental level. It is possible to use creative visualization to connect universal archetypes to this subtle body. The images and their location in our body are not chosen randomly, but according to a structure and a code given by tradition. This code is part of revelations given during an initiatory process in respected schools such as the Aurum Solis. If we use the same layout, it is possible to connect these different planes and attract a higher and more powerful energy. Channeling energy like so is an excellent way to change our lives for the better.

THE CAUSAL BODY

We are now reaching what we might call the soul. This body is very rarely accessible to the observer, whether in training or not. It is necessary to reach a high level of consciousness to have access to this essential part of what we are.

It is very difficult to describe this subtle body. Unlike the previous parts of occult anatomy, it is independent from the physical world and has no dense manifestation. It is not, strictly speaking, related to the physical body at all, but belongs to the spiritual plane. It was created in the divine world and never embodied. It generated the other subtle bodies for specific functions but remained separated.

Description

We can say that at the beginning of its development, the mental body had a spherical shape sometimes associated with colors and specific shapes. But the causal body is structured according to archetypal principles, so it appears as a symbolic, geometric shape. The causal body is the reflection of the divine spark that can be found in most human beings. It is surrounded by a halo of a specific color that becomes visible a short distance away from the edge of this body. To someone fully dedicated to spirituality who has achieved a certain level of awareness, the main color is often white or golden. Very rarely, some other color can be seen instead of these. Shapes may vary from a sphere to a diamond, or to even more complex formations by combination of various geometric structures.

It is important to remember that although the causal body cannot be seen during training, the archetypal structures it generates can be found on the mental plane. It is more common that one feels this body rather than observes it directly. Indeed, the infinite goodness or radiance emanating from an adept is more perceptible than a direct vision of the causal body.

Function

The causal body is similar to a jewelry case, a repository of what has been kept during previous incarnations. Unlike the mental body, the causal body only records the highest, most spiritual parts of our human life. In the beginning, the causal body emanated from a cosmic principle. Consequently, our essence can be seen as divine. As human beings, we've lost the ability to see and communicate with this highest level of who we are. We must practice a psychic and spiritual training to connect to this reality. It is not true that this causal body is immortal and already perfect; as a matter of fact, the causal body grows and evolves. Everything great, noble, and true reaches this plane and contributes to its edification and growth. Then it constitutes itself as a body of light that moves from incarnation to incarnation. This causal body, hidden in the core of our aura, is a seed of strength, courage, and inspiration. Someone who walks the spiritual path and expresses empathy to their fellow humans is following the impulses received from their causal body. However, it is up to the individual to accept or decline this call.

Annie Besant explains that only good spiritual thoughts are assimilated into this causal body, allowing it to grow in light during life. However, perverse thoughts and tendencies can be recorded in the causal body during the death process, when astral and mental envelopes are dissolved.[5] Patricia's and my observations, as well as those coming from other Western adepts, have not confirmed this statement. But as you can see, this philosophy is very far from the Judeo-Christian doctrines of hell and purgatory—it includes no vengeful god, no eternal sufferings; only our actions and their consequences are considered here.

The development of the causal body and its survival must therefore be the main objective of our life. Living according to high moral standards is one of the best ways to achieve this goal. As you develop psychic abilities such as astral vision with the exercises in this book, keep this goal always in the back of your mind. No positive action is lost. Everything positive contributes to the development of your being and to the emergence of the most advanced stages of mindfulness.

The causal body is also the place where your consciousness will move to survive death. This supreme spiritual work is the goal of advanced theurgic work in authentic initiatory Orders such as the Aurum Solis. Eventually, the manifestation of the causal body will be a fundamental stage of this journey.

5. Besant, *Man and His Bodies.*

Chapter Two
MAPPING THE DIVINE ARCHETYPES

In the 1990s, as I was investigating specific aspects of the aura, I had a strange experience that opened a whole new world to me. This revelation brought teachings I had received a long time ago to light for the first time. Sometimes simple things are taught and written without giving much explanation. Only after months and years of experimentation do we understand something that was obvious all the time.

Everything started with a fraternal conversation at the end of a Masonic meeting. A Masonic brother and I were seated in a Masonic lodge, talking about symbols and history. Freemasons like to chat and many are interested in traditions and great mysteries. Everyone had left the building and the place was quiet. Most of the lights had been turned off. Only the soft ceiling lighting still shone. The conversation turned to the soul and the astral body. My brother knew that I was doing extensive research and training in this area. After more than an hour of conversation, he convinced me to read his aura, something I wouldn't normally do in this context. However, the time was good, the place peaceful, and the light perfect. I agreed to go ahead. We installed a new seat in front of me for my friend. I have to say, conditions were almost ideal, and as I love silence, it was even better.

After breathing and relaxing, I started to use what I call "stereo vision" to see the etheric body. It took a few seconds. The size of the body was what it should be. The color was a little shinier than usual, which is normal after attending a ritual and taking several minutes to focus on breathing.

Then I changed my vision to reach the astral aura. Here again, the effects of the ritual were easy to perceive. In this case, lights and colors are brighter; they move more slowly and the harmony is greater. It is always a pleasure to see auras like that—it gives a feeling of happy relaxation and peace. I was silently contemplating these fascinating streams of light flowing through the aura. The main chakras were rotating with different speeds and colors. Without analyzing too much, I watched these movements linking the three bodies—physical, etheric, and astral. The circulation of energy was regular. I don't know why, but this vision and the emotion linked to it reminded me of some fascinating mountain streams I'd seen during my last hike. I was seated in front of my brother and yet I was in the mountains watching this regenerative flow at the same time.

Then, as my concentration weakened a little, small dots of energy appeared around the body. At the same time, another very luminous aura that I recognized as the mental aura unveiled its specific shape. These dots, concentrations of energy, gathered into radiant spheres of various colors. As incredible as it may seem, they started to exchange energies of a higher frequency than the aura. Each specific color was contained in these transparent spheres, surrounded by a luminous nimbus. A complex exchange of energies was happening between them. Everything was brighter, more subtle, and more aerial than the aura.

Following these beautiful and mysterious manifestations, I focused on a vermillion-red sphere that seemed to me the most luminous. It was located around the right shoulder of my friend. For a moment, I saw only the red color becoming clearer and then, as if via zoom, my gaze moved into the sphere. A scene appeared in front of a reddish background. A mighty warrior was standing on a chariot pulled by a brown horse. The figure wore a helmet surmounted by a mane. His gaze was resolute. A metal breastplate sat over a red tunic. His right hand held a javelin. Whistling noises surrounded the scene, and dark, red clouds roamed the sky. While I watched the scene unfold, I felt a considerable influx of energy. It was a peaceful power, but very intense. Then suddenly everything stopped, and I returned to a peripheral vision of all the bright spheres in my friend's mental aura. Everything had lasted only a few seconds, and I realized that these centers belonged to a reality other than the one I saw in his aura. The spheres were present in the mental aura, a place they should not have been. As for the image appearing in the sphere itself, it was the symbolic representation of a specific power belonging to the causal plane. This "magic" image was a manifestation of the causal plane and a door to access it.

The ten spheres pulsated slightly in front of me, some brighter than others. As I was examining the structure as a whole, I realized that I was looking at the famous Kabbalistic tree. It was there all the time, but only revealed when my astral vision reached the mental plane. It was not a secret that my friend had been learning Kabbalah for a few years and actively practiced Kabbalistic rituals. What I was seeing was one of the effects of this spiritual work.

The structure of the Tree of Life is well-known to those who are interested in Kabbalah, although they may not know that it can exist within the psychic bodies. After contemplating this occult structure, I started to breathe and release my vision of this plane. Going down to the astral aura, I saw a halo at the location of each sphere, so transparent that I hadn't seen it when I began.

Needless to say, my friend was very surprised to hear about this vision, and even more so when I highlighted the predominance of the red sphere. As a matter of fact, he explained to me, he was currently working on Geburah, a sefira linked to the red planet, Mars.

Over the following weeks and months, I explored several auras to see if this Kabbalistic pattern existed universally, or at least in those I was able to observe. This was not the case. It was visible only in the aura of those who were actively learning this tradition. Instead, other geometrical structures were visible, and sometimes I saw scenes difficult to connect with anything I knew.

In chapter 2, we mentioned that many descriptions of subtle bodies can be found. Most of the time, they are very close and we can see their similarities and connections, although the number of bodies often differs. In some cases, the numbers are impossible to reconcile. We must admit that such discrepancy is very troubling and empowers skeptics. Either what we can see is true and common, or it is not. Although our physical bodies can be different colors, their general appearance is similar, and logic would seem to indicate that this should be true of the subtle bodies as well. We should not ignore the fact that the auras described in this text have been described in many different ways, depending on the period or culture in which the description originates. The experience just shared with you should help connect the dots.

THE MENTAL BODY

As previously explained, the mental body does not have any definitive structure. Indeed, its brightness is usually so intense that focusing on specific areas can be very challenging. Structures are present, but of an unusual kind; the level of energy and its vibrations are much higher than the etheric and astral bodies. They do not behave in the same way. Let's highlight three principles of the mental body: First, it is linked to divine archetypes belonging to the causal plane. Second, it is malleable and takes a specific organization according to the inner work or beliefs of the individual. Third, it affects our way of thinking, our beliefs, the astral aura, and even our entire life.

Let's examine each of these three principles.

Independence from the Lower Planes

The centers of the mental body are bridges between the mental plane and the causal plane. The latter is similar to the divine plane, the pure realm of ideas described by the philosopher Plato. They are pure abstractions separated from the multiple appearances of the world we live in. The general concept of a tree is a good example. As soon as we hear the word *tree*, we envision different varieties of trees. However, all are still part of the general idea of "tree." You can apply the same reasoning to the sun or a geometric shape like a triangle. When we consider the archetypes as a source of energy generated on the causal plane, we can easily understand that they can connect to a mental structure, but not in the subtle bodies closer to the physical body. This causal plane remains beyond our human thought, but occult anatomy is not separated from this plane. We possess a causal body, the presence of the divine in us, which is necessarily related to the plane it belongs to.

Malleability

This is one of the most important concepts. The archetypes are, above all, ideas made of pure energy and cannot be seen in their true forms. As stated in the first principle, they are present in the mental body only as shapeless energy. This energy is affected by our mind, spiritual work, and religious and philosophical beliefs. That is why the Kabbalistic ritual work of my friend organized this energy in the shape of the Kabbalistic tree. What would have happened if he instead practiced Enochian magic, or Wicca, or was attending Catholic Mass every Sunday? Would the Kabbalistic tree still have been in his aura? As a matter of fact, the answer is no. Regular practices and strong beliefs organize the energy of the mental body according to the representation of the cosmos. A theosophist, a kabbalist, a theurgist, or a yogi are all developing a different organization of this energy that can often be depicted as a map.

Effect

As explained in the previous aura reading, the sefirot spheres of the Kabbalistic tree were hardly visible in the astral aura. Without having the full vision of the mental aura, it was almost impossible to notice them. Since this experience, I have had many opportunities to confirm their presence in the lower subtle bodies of this hidden structure. The energy is flowing through these centers, as invisible and real as a black hole in the cosmos. There is something mysterious and fascinating in this phenomenon. Subtle bodies being made of energy are all interconnected; if one is affected by something, the other ones will be too. We see that such natural organization of the subtle bodies exists. However, the astral aura, the etheric, and even sometimes the physical body are affected by this inner structure.

Here are two examples to illustrate this process. In the example of Kabbalah given earlier, the energy was structured by the ritual work according to the Kabbalistic Tree. Such a spiritual map is linked with archetypes of the same tradition. This is what is called an *egregore*. Then the mental body is empowered by this specific energy. The energy will start to radiate in the lower bodies through the sefirotic centers present in the aura. The astral aura will be affected, changing the mood and reaction of the believer. Consequently, colors could change, or the individual could feel the need to change their diet according to the Kabbalistic tradition, etc. When a more advanced knowledge is involved, the subtle bodies themselves can be combined in a different way.

What we just explained for a practitioner of Kabbalah will be the same for a yoga teacher, a Wiccan, or a theurgist. As you may realize now, we have freedom to choose our spiritual path, but this choice will have huge consequences! Our auras can reorganize while following a spiritual path and training our psychic abilities.

It is true that archetypes are universal, but their representation and our understanding can be different. Nevertheless, this universality and the laws of the cosmos give a direction to the occult anatomy of all human beings. As long as we are unaware of this occult process, the organization of our subtle bodies is almost the same; the only small differences are coming from our culture. Some of us are also affected by past lives and, eventually, by practices and beliefs. In the first chapters of the book, we have presented what most of us have in common: the subtle bodies, their structure, and their organization can be considered similar. However, we evolve and many things can change.

Some archetypes that have existed and created an egregore remain very powerful today. They belong to systems that are followed by millions of practitioners and believers. Their power is undeniable and cannot be ignored. Some of these egregores are expanding and others are shrinking. Obviously, they do not affect everyone in the same way. There is a difference between practicing yoga, attending yoga workshops, or becoming a yoga teacher. This is true for other practices and beliefs as well. Some spiritual maps have emerged at the beginning of the twenty-first century as more powerful than others but, as expected, most are coming from the past, and it is essential to highlight their characteristics.

THE KABBALISTIC MAP

In the Hebrew Kabbalah, the Universe is divided into four worlds: Assiah (the material plane), Yetzirah (the astral plane), Briah (the mental plane), and Atziluth (the divine plane).

The occult structure of human beings is closely related to these planes, even if it exceeds them. Externally, the soul reflects the structure of the sefirot, and internally, the divine light. This reflection of the divine is called *Demut Elohim*.

Keep in mind that such a long tradition has developed several interpretations that can be different in detail; we should expect such differences, as the egregore has its own way to understand God and everything he created. Without going into the twists and turns of Kabbalah, we can highlight the main aspects of these four subtle bodies and the world they belong to.

Assiah, the Material World, and Nephesh

Assiah corresponds to the physical world. It is the material manifestation of the powers of the upper worlds. The complexity and apparent chaos of this world might surprise you. Yet, appearances can be deceiving. The world containing the microcosm and macrocosm corresponds to the sefirot Chesed, Geburah, Tiphareth, Netzach, Hod, and Yesod.

According to the famous Kabbalistic text called the *Zohar*, when you were born, God gave you a *nephesh*. This is the lowest level of consciousness. It is the life force of the body. Literally, nephesh is the soul, but more precisely, "life." Obviously, you could compare the nephesh to the circulation of prana in our etheric body. Some authors characterize the nephesh as the physiological function of the body. The etheric observed during the training can be related to the nephesh. As a matter of fact, it is really the intermediary between matter and subtle bodies.

Yetzirah, the Astral World, and Ruach

Yetzirah corresponds to the astral plane. It is the origin of the world of appearances in which we live. Everything that occurs in the physical world takes place in Yetzirah first. However, Yetzirah is subject to modifications and remains indeterminate and changeable. It is the recipient of an abundance of pictures emanating from Assiah, many of which constitute our emotions. This world corresponds to the sefirot Kether, Chokmah, and Binah.

The second subtle body defined in Kabbalah is called *ruach*. Its main manifestations are emotions such as love, hate, anger, and desire. We can say that it is the emotional soul, the place where human urges emerge. It can distinguish between good and evil.

Briah, the Mental World, and Neshama

Briah corresponds to the world of creation, which contains the archetypal pictures of creation but not the archetypes themselves. The mental world contains the pictures of the realities, which are visible to anyone who is able to perceive this plane. It is necessary to differentiate those pictures that manifest themselves in Briah; those pictures are part of the world of Yetzirah. In Yetzirah, there are numerous changeable pictures that have their origin in the emotions associated with Assiah. In Briah, the pictures are the lower reflection of the archetypal realities of Atziluth. This world corresponds to the sefirot Kether, Chokmah, and Binah.

In the human microcosm, Briah is related to rational consciousness, the energies of being, and the subtle body called *neshama*. Neshama is the intellectual soul and reason. This subtle body contains the divine sparks received when we were born. As such, it survives after death and ascends to higher realms.

Atziluth, the Divine World, and Chaya

Archetypes are found in this world of pure abstraction. The archetypal principles of the Kabbalistic Tree are also found in this world. The seven traditional planets relate to these spheres. This world corresponds to the sefira Kether.

In the human microcosm, Atziluth is related to the spiritual soul, the superconscious, and archetypal principles. It is called the *Chaya*. It gives one the consciousness of the divine power.

Yechida

Yechida is the highest level, only reached by a few adepts and initiates. This level of consciousness allows our spirit to contemplate God, reaching the divine essence, *Ain Soph*, which we cannot comprehend with our reason.

Above the four worlds, Kabbalists teach the existence of three "veils of negative existence," which are Ain Soph Aur (infinite light), Ain Soph (the infinite), and Ain (the nothing).

The Tree of Life

As explained previously, the sefirot may appear in the aura under specific conditions, including your culture and religion, psychic training, or spiritual practices. According to this tradition, they are related to the world of creation. Each sefira corresponds to symbols, parts of the body, states of consciousness, and characteristics of our being. If you work with this system or observe the aura of a Kabbalist, it will be beneficial to provide the keywords to help you in your investigations, no matter your level.

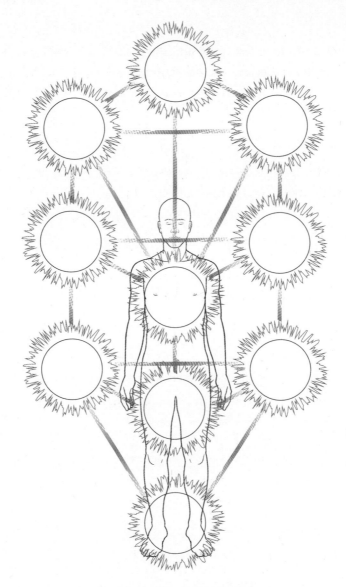

Manifestation of the Kabbalistic Tree in
the Subtle Bodies of a Kabbalist

The ten spheres are organized according to a pattern that looks like a tree when seen from the front or back. They are not placed on a flat surface; each sphere has several levels or refractions, but it is not useful to explain every detail here. Let's summarize each sefira, starting from the highest sphere.

Kether

The first sphere to manifest itself, and the highest of all, is called Kether, or "crown." It is the archetypal manifestation of the origin of the deity. It is a pure concentration of light energy, potentially containing all that is to come. It is the perfect unit.

Strength: Unity

Body: Skull

Cosmic Symbol: Spiral nebula

Archetypal or Magic Image: Old, bearded king seen in profile

Chokmah

The second sphere, Chokmah, or "wisdom," represents paternity. It is the place in which energy increases and accelerates.

Strength: Expansion

Body: Right brain

Cosmic Symbol: Sphere of the fixed stars

Archetypal or Magic Image: Bearded patriarch

Binah

The third sphere is Binah, or "understanding." It corresponds to the feminine power—maternity. It gives a form to everything that will exist and pass through it. It channels the energies that flow through it.

Strength: Constriction

Body: Left brain

Cosmic Symbol: Saturn

Archetypal or Magic Image: Heavenly queen

Archetypal Meaning: Unchangeable stability

Modern Color: Indigo

Chesed

The fourth sphere, Chesed, or "kindness," has an expansive character that prepares a transition from the abstract to the concrete. It expresses an attenuated form of paternity present in Chokmah. It takes the place of the legislator and expresses kindness in a second form, called Gedulah.

Strength: Order

Body: Right arm

Cosmic Symbol: Jupiter

Archetypal or Magic Image: Priest-king on his throne

Archetypal Meaning: Majestic benevolence

Modern Color: Blue

Geburah

The fifth sphere, Geburah, or "discipline," is an expression of divine justice and strength.

Strength: Energy

Body: Left arm

Cosmic Symbol: Mars

Archetypal or Magic Image: Warrior-king in arms

Archetypal Meaning: Intrepid strength

Modern Color: Red

Tiphareth

The sixth sphere, Tiphareth, or "beauty," expresses harmony, beauty, and balance. It is the place of passage and exchange between the forces from above and from below. It gathers the qualities and energy of Kether.

Strength: Balance

Body: Torso

Cosmic Symbol: Sun

Archetypal or Magic Image: Divine child; solar king; sacrificed god

Archetypal Meaning: Fertile splendor

Modern Color: Yellow

Netzach

The seventh sphere, Netzach, or "victory," allows love and vitality to manifest itself in the world of form, or in natural existence.

Strength: Combination

Body: Right leg

Cosmic Symbol: Venus

Archetypal or Magic Image: Naked Amazon

Archetypal Meaning: Celestial love

Modern Color: Green

Hod

The eighth sphere, Hod, or "glory," divides and analyzes. It corresponds to the intellectual dimension.

Strength: Separation

Body: Left leg

Cosmic Symbol: Mercury

Archetypal or Magic Image: Hermaphrodite

Archetypal Meaning: Spirit of wisdom

Modern Color: Orange

Yesod

The ninth sphere, Yesod, or "foundation," expresses the divine force through the changing and multiple forms of this world. The effects on the physical plane can be manifested from it.

Strength: Conception

Body: Sexual organs

Cosmic Symbol: Moon

Archetypal or Magic Image: Ithyphallic young man

Archetypal Meaning: Change and to become

Modern Color: Violet

Malkuth

The tenth sphere, Malkuth, or "kingship," expresses fulfillment and interaction between things. It is composed of the four elements.

Strength: Resolution

Body: Mouth

Cosmic Symbol: Earth

Archetypal or Magic Image: Veiled young women

Archetypal Meaning: Stability and silence

Modern Color: Spectrum of the seven colors

Three Columns

The ten spheres are also organized in three vertical columns, giving a specific meaning that is added to the character already defined for each of them. They are:

Left Column (Binah, Geburah, Hod): Rigor, feminine

Right Column (Chokmah, Chesed, Netzach): Mercy, masculine

Central Column (Kether, Tiphareth, Yesod, Malkuth): Balance or mildness, bisexual or neutral

Sefirot and Chakras

Some connections with the chakras are obvious and interesting to mention, in particular:

- Kether and sahasrara (crown)
- Binah is sometimes associated with ajna (third eye)
- Da'ath and vishuddha (throat)
- Tiphareth and anahata (heart)

• Yesod and svadhishthana (sacral)

• Malkuth and muladhara (root)

Other secondary chakras could also be associated with sefirot, but that would take us too far.

THE HERMETIC MAP

Hermeticism and theurgy have been taught and practiced for hundreds of years. Occult anatomy has actively been used in rituals by authentic initiatory Orders dating back from this origin. This is especially the case for the Aurum Solis.[6] As heads of this famous tradition, we have actively talked about this structure. In recent years, it has been used by more people, increasing its power and light. It is interesting to highlight that, contrary to Kabbalah, this tradition uses principles and sacred books that have never been used to threaten anyone. Consequently, the egregore has kept an impressive purity that makes it very safe to use.

The occult anatomy is structured according to five parts:

1. The body (*Soma*)
2. The bodies of light (*Hepithumia—Ochema*)
3. The soul (*Psuche*)
4. The spirit or intellect (*Nous*)
5. The divine aspect (*Theos*)

I have extensively explained each one in a previous book called *Rediscover the Magick of the Gods and Goddesses*, but I will provide a summary of the main elements of each part here. This summary will give you all the necessary elements to explain what could be observed in the aura of a Hermetist.

The Body (Soma)

Our body is the material part of what we are. Its structure and shape are organized according to the principles provided by the spirit (nous). The five elements are combined to organize our organism. This physical body is dif-

6. See www.aurumsolis.org for more information.

ferent than the essence of our being. The goal is to transcend this physical limitation.

The Bodies of Light (Hepithumia—Ochema)

The first of these subtle bodies, the etheric, is called the *thumos* in Platonic theology.

The aura is closely associated with the luminous body, ochema, which is the vehicle of the soul. This invisible and luminous body of the soul is made of aetheric material. Once perfected, it is often compared to a starry vehicle. It is literally the "astral body." It allows the soul to descend into the body without being under the dominion of the flesh. The ochema is sometimes called the *pneuma* (breath). Ochema is not derived from the physical body. This vehicle is very subtle.

In your observation, you may also find a sort of reflection of this luminous body. This reflection is not a pure illusion. It is a manifestation of the ochema, called an *Eidôlon* in Platonic theology. It is also bonded to the physical and emotional bodies (soma and thumos), and as such, is always drawn toward their terrestrial inclinations.

The Soul (Psuche)

Simply said, "you" are the soul (psuche). This is the spiritual and individual part of us, which is the origin of our individual creativity and awareness. It is the soul that unifies our memories in a coherent way and organizes them into an inner self. This soul came from above and contains the memories of our previous lives. After having completed our current life, the psuche will travel again to the outer world before returning in another body. Hopefully, if we are lucky or well trained, we will return with a good part of our memories intact. Our souls are immortal and independent from the material world.

The Spirit (Nous)

The nous is often used as a synonym for intelligence, awareness, and intellect. However, the nous is not the part of us that does discursive reasoning. The nous is the ability to reason itself, or the intellect, but not the active process of deciding. Reasonable speech is the servant of the nous. Reasonable speech comes from inner silence.

It is interesting to highlight that Hermetists explain that every human being has a body (soma) and a soul (psuche), but not every soul has an intellect (nous). There is a divine part of the nous and another one (less divine) that belongs to the soul.

The nous is a fundamental articulation of the spiritual life. In the *Corpus Hermeticum*, it says: "Agathodaimon said that the Soul is in your body, the Nous in your Soul, the Word in your Nous, and God is the father of all that." Later, the same text states: "The most subtle part of the Soul is the Nous, and for the Nous this is God."[7]

The Divine (Theos)

In Greek, *theos* means "God." The upper part of the nous is the highest and the more subtle part of our being. It is the real presence of the divine, of God, inside us. This is a divine presence that we can imagine as a light, hidden at the top of our inner self and showing us the way.

THE KEMETIC MAP

The religious tradition of ancient Egypt never really disappeared. Large parts have been associated to the Hermetic and theurgic tradition that we just discussed. Various teachings were also incorporated in famous Greek schools, such as Pythagorism and Platonism. We must remember that both Pythagoras and Plato spent several years in the Egyptian temples.

Besides these two main channels, philosophical and initiatory, an interest in Egypt was revived and reborn after the military campaign of Napoleon Bonaparte in this country at the end of the eighteenth century. Scientists, artists, and archaeologists who travelled with him came back with hundreds of documents that would eventually help Champollion to decipher the ancient language. At the same time, Freemasons, who were a part of the same campaign, re-created Egyptian rituals within their tradition. This history and its rituals are presented in my book *Esoteric Freemasonry*. This Egyptian freemasonry has survived and is still practiced in several countries.

In the eighties, another movement was started to revive the religious aspect of ancient Egypt. Today, it is identified as *Kemetism*. Most of its follow-

---

7. De Biasi, *Rediscover the Magick of the Gods and Goddesses*, 151–52.

ers pursue this religious path. However, other practitioners, often linked to initiatory Orders and sometimes freemasonry, practice a more magical path. This tradition has always been very powerful. The occult anatomy, which was developed alongside centuries of Egyptian tradition, is very much alive and can transform our subtle bodies. It is still a mystery how fast such modifications can occur in the aura of someone practicing these rituals, which is why it is important to share these elements with you.

The Body and Its Mummy

The sculptor who gives life, named Khnum, created *khat*, a child's body.[8] From conception to death, the Egyptian view of the body was mostly magical. After the body transformed into a mummy, a Sah (sahu) had to undergo the Opening of the Mouth ceremony to have its senses restored, as the body had to justify itself before the judges of the underworld.

The sahu has been variously described as the spirit-body, a self-defined psychic boundary, or the repository of the soul. It was seemingly immortal and similar in form to the mortal body.

The Heart

A special part of the body was the heart, the essence of life and seat of the mind with its emotions, intelligence, and moral sense. The heart gave man's life direction. Enjoyment was closely tied to the sensations of the body. Following one's heart meant living a full life.

During embalming, the heart was not removed with the other interior organs. Instead, a scarab was inserted into the mummy's bindings right above the heart to prevent it from speaking out against its owner. It's interesting to mention that, during an aura reading of a real practitioner of this tradition, I could see amulets pulsing randomly. This was one of the strange effects of the malleability of the mental aura and the power of this ancient tradition.

The Ka

Unfortunately, the ancient Egyptians never clearly defined what was meant by the *ka*, or its female complementary, the *hemset*. The concepts may have

---

8. De Biasi and Bourin, *The Ultimate Pagan Almanac 2019*.

undergone changes over the millennia or had different meanings according to the social settings. Ka has been variously translated as "soul," "life force," "will," etc., but no single Western concept is anything like it. The closest to it in the English language may be a "life-creating force."

The ka was a constant close companion of the body in life and death, depicted throughout the pharaonic period following the king and bearing the royal Horus name. The ka came into being when a person was born, often depicted as a twin or a double. Unlike the body it belonged to, it was immortal if provided with proper nourishment. Being a spiritual entity, it did not eat food but seems to have extracted life-sustaining forces from offerings, be they real or symbolic. The ka has also been interpreted as the "protecting divine spirit" that survived the death of the body. It can also remain embodied in a statue or a picture of the deceased.

In the 1980s I travelled to Egypt for a couple of months. As many tourists do, I visited the Cairo Museum and the famous mummies of the great kings of Egypt. I can assure you that these mummies were not dead! Standing still and opening my astral vision revealed a very different reality—colors, waves of light, even pulsations of energy were surrounding the corpses. It was not a manifestation of a living being per se, but a type of living energy maintaining a certain level of consciousness. Strangely, my first reactions were admiration and love. I was deeply moved by this invisible presence and this manifestation of immortality. Later, I had an opportunity to see mummies in Italy and France, but I never experienced the same manifestation. Undoubtedly, ancient Egyptian priests knew how to see and handle subtle bodies. These mysteries are still taught in some mystery schools to this day.

The Shadow

In the light of the life-giving sun, body and shadow were inseparable. But this "shadow" was not an ordinary shadow of a body. Rather, it belonged to the world of the "soul," moving independently of its body and partaking of the funerary offerings. Unlike the body, the shadow was not bound to the grave and could go anywhere the body could not.

Ren

The notion of secret words or names was very important in ancient Egypt. It remains a key element of some initiatory Orders of the Western tradition. Such a name given at birth to Egyptians was kept secret; only a nickname was used in public life. The survival of the soul depends on the existence of ren.

The Ba

The ba was the sum of the immortal forces inherent in human beings, making up their personality. It has been called a person's psyche and is generally translated as "soul." But it was also considered a corporeal, sexual being, which needed food and drink.

The ba was mostly represented in the form of a bird, generally with a human head and, according to grave images, often perching on trees planted by the tomb. It moved about, sometimes in the company of the shadow, but did not stray far. Every evening it returned to the body, reuniting, and thus ensuring the body's continued existence in the afterlife.

The Akh

The akh belongs to heaven, the corpse to earth. The body is buried while the akh, the Shining One, ascended to the sky and transformed into a star. It came into being when ba and ka united and was the part of the person least bound to the rest, leaving it behind in the quest for immortality.

The pharaoh, symbolic representation of an adept, having a divine nature, had always become an akh and joined the stars after the demise of his mortal shell. However, according to the later Old Kingdom, ordinary mortals could also attain this status when they became transfigured dead. Akh has been translated as "spirit," "ghost," or "transfiguration." Sekhem is also a distinct part of the akh; sekhem can be seen as a life energy for the soul.

Chapter Three
GENESIS OF THE AURA

Bodies of light grow and develop as the physical body does. The process begins before birth. Few texts on the aura deal with the important period of pregnancy, but the development of a human being in the womb is fascinating on both the physical and spiritual levels. After developing your psychic ability, you will be able to observe the aura during pregnancy. The methods in this chapter are what Patricia and I did, using the teachings received from famous initiatory Orders and ancient authors.

We must start by highlighting the close connection between the physical body's development and that of the subtle bodies. The latter generate the occult structure of energy that is the foundation of the physical body. The physical process that occurs when sperm meets the egg are well-known today, but the inherent memory of matter guiding this cellular "intelligence" is less well-known. Specific information is present in the DNA of the cell. However, this does not fully explain the emergence of consciousness in human beings. Some unexplained memories that arise at a young age cannot always be explained by cell memory. From this, we deduce that something else exists outside of the physical plane and is added to it.

As a matter of fact, everything starts very early, when the egg starts growing, dividing into many cells. At this moment a nucleus of energy comes to life. It generates an extremely active and dynamic etheric substance using a high level of pure prana. This energy is projected around the core in the form of filaments of light. Like solar rays, red, gold, and blue filaments emanate from this ovum. The multiplication of cells follows the emergence of this web of energy. This kind of weaving occurs until the three specialized layers of the embryo are obtained. The inner layer produces the respiratory system, digestive system, and glands. The middle layer structures bones, muscles, kidneys, and the circulatory system. The outer layer creates the nervous system, skin, hair, nails, and tooth enamel. All these specific processes bring energy to each physical body part as it develops.

The etheric energy, while weaving the organs before they become visible physically, begins to organize the channels of energies, the nadis, which ensure its good circulation. Then the chakras, the most important energy centers, appear and intensify the circulation of energy even more. As the chakras become more active, a form of consciousness begins to appear. At this stage of development, only the etheric, astral, and pranic energies are active. A phenomenon occurs around the fourth month, after the main chakras are established. A very intense and vivid channel of light springs from the fetus to the astral plane. In response to this flash, another beam of light descends into the channel toward the fetus.

The energies involved until this moment are still too limited to organize the physical vehicle in a coherent way. The memory and experience of past lives are needed. The creation of this channel of light allows the soul still on the astral plane to bring down some of its energy into the new body. Usually, this descent of energy occurs through the crown chakra.

Then, the soul descends into the body and begins to work. It weaves the different subtle bodies according to its karmic memory and the conditions of the physical organism. It works to combine and balance the genetic heritage and its own karmic inheritance. Indeed, our human heredity has a certain malleability, and it is the soul that influences the physical body in one direction rather than another.

We want to emphasize the fact that this period is extremely important for the soul's work. It is therefore necessary for the mother and the father to have a peaceful daily life, exempt of stress, to allow a harmonious organization. During this period, the mother should avoid discordant noises and music, as well as bright and aggressive artificial lights. She should reduce the quantity of food she consumes and cut or reduce all kinds of stimulants. In fact, she should find the best ways to purify her body, both mentally and physically.

However, she should maintain moderation. A pregnant woman should not underfeed herself but should avoid any excess during this period. This practice will help the soul perform its task as effectively as possible. This balance, along with the mother's positive thoughts, create powerful energies used by the soul to structure the subtle bodies.

The process continues with the full development of the different subtle bodies, assisted by beings from spiritual planes. Some authors have identified these beings as angels, but such terminology is too closely related to religious doctrines to be a correct description.

At this point, it appears that the mental body is still in its infant stages, although a slightly shining ovoid shape is already visible. The wheels of energy are still being built. At this point, the causal body is slightly larger than the mental body. The whole body is immersed in a magnificent bright light. The intensity of the light is higher toward the center of the causal body.

The psychic and physical development continue according to the occult structure organized by the soul. The different bodies become more distinct, while the brain and major physical functions are established.

By the sixth month, the organization of the whole body is well advanced. Memories of past lives have helped to create a vehicle for the soul suitable for the upcoming life. It is sometimes possible to observe miniature scenes belonging to the past lives in the aura of the fetus images. These sequences seem to form on the surface of the mental aura and dissolve into its luminosity, merging with it. Careful observations of this process show that not all of these visual memories dissolve. Some get smaller and smaller, shrinking instead of dissolving. This is the mark of memories that will not totally disappear. Consequently, it is possible to access this part of the occult structure if necessary. To be successful in such work, a practitioner would need both a high level of competence and a very good reason.

It is also possible to observe variously colored filaments of light in the aura. They emerge from the subtle bodies of the fetus and shine outward, going beyond the body of the mother. If we follow these waves of light, we may discover within a radius of six to ten feet one or more creatures, invisible to the physical eye, helping develop the various bodies. These spiritual beings have several functions. They are present to protect this new creature and support its harmonious development. We should note that such angelic beings have many roles that are not limited to the current task.

Sometimes, before a baby is born, we can observe a particular phenomenon. The current of light that exists between the high levels of the psychic worlds and the fetus becomes a place of an intense movement. Bright waves of energy circulate inside this "tube." The energy waves represent an exchange of information between the spiritual and physical planes. Then, a strong energy appears a short distance from the mother, sometimes in the form of a sphere. This light enters the physical and auric body of the fetus through this channel of light. At the same time, the original channel that allowed energies to circulate is absorbed and disappears.

Only the fetus's auras and the chakras already created remain visible. The crown chakra, positioned where the channel previously connected, is now radiating. The energy now comes mainly from the fetus. The spirit and the self are now in the body. Generally, birth occurs in the days following these phenomena. The memories of the infant's past lives, any psychic abilities, and the power of the aura remain present, supporting the new life to come.

It is important to remember the role of the mother and the environment she created during the pregnancy. Everything contributes to the development of the child's potential. Her responsibility is not limited to the physical body; she also has a responsibility to help this new human being remain aware of past lives and be ready for this one. She should cultivate beauty, love, and purity. These are the main elements the soul needs to build harmonious and healthy bodies.

Chapter Four

THE AURA AND
ELECTROPHOTOGRAPHY

This book is based on oral traditions and direct observations. Hundreds of workshops and trainings have enabled Patricia and I to verify the efficiency of these techniques. However, although our process is rigorous, it is not scientific per se; it has not been scientifically verified and demonstrated. We could wait to share our techniques until science explores this field and develops the necessary tools for an easy examination of the aura, but we don't know when that will happen. So, we move forward, welcoming any new discoveries along the way.

It's important to note that several discoveries and experimentations already took place in the eighteenth and twentieth centuries. They reinforce what we have personally observed, as well as many teachings from different spiritual schools. This chapter will discuss these discoveries and the history of electrophotography as I have learned it over the last thirty years.

Between 1940 and 1960, a method for photographing the aura was discovered. This method is called *Kirlian photography*, after its Russian inventors. From what we know about the subtle bodies, Kirlian photography detects the etheric body, not the astral aura itself. This discovery is still fascinating, and the photos are mesmerizing.

It all goes back to an important eighteenth-century figure named Mesmer. Mesmer used an invisible power he called "animal magnetism" to perform group therapy using various devices. The most popular was a large wooden bathtub connected to copper wires touched by the participants. This process concentrated the vital energy of the patients and triggered strong reactions, leading in many cases to a cure (or at least a remission) of their diseases.[9] At the beginning of the nineteenth century, Carl von Reichenbach also studied vital energy and human emanations. He called this power the "Odic force," or OD. Renowned British chemists and physicists William Crookes and Edward William Cox investigated these human magnetic fluids as well.

The first modes of electrophotography in America and Europe appeared at the end of the nineteenth century. In 1842 an Englishman named Carsten used an electric condenser to obtain reproductions of coins on a sheet of mica. It seems that the Russian M. F. Crestin did the same in 1894, using a photographic plate placed on a tin sheet connected to the positive pole of this system. The coin was placed directly on the surface of the photographic plate, and the negative pole was in contact with the coin.

In 1880, Nikola Tesla carried out experiments on the electric field. He succeeded in making the electricity surrounding an individual visible as a crown of luminous flames. Around this time, a Russian researcher named Yakov Narkevich-Todka carried out similar electrophotography experiments.[10]

In the late 1800s, a Polish citizen named J. J. Narkiewiecz and a Czech named Barthélémy Navratil experimented with electrophotography and took thousands of photos. They studied and experimented under various conditions such as polarities, exposure times, electrodes, etc. In 1965 the Czech Encyclopedia published some of these photographs. Many books, magazines, and exhibitions of the time presented their work. However, the images were considered more as artistic creations than useful photos providing a new understanding of human beings. Very few considered these experiments to be something serious and useful from a scientific standpoint.

It was in 1939 with Semyon and Valentina Kirlian that serious research really started. The Kirlians were the first to experiment with a rigorous and methodical protocol using a device they created. History reports that Semyon had the idea to build such a device when, while working as an electrician,

---

9. Turner, "Mesmeromania."

10. "History."

he observed a blue flame between a patient's skin and a glass electrode. This device was used at that time to treat rheumatism via high electronic frequencies. The parameters used were high frequency, high voltage, low amperage. He developed this technique by creating a device that could offer the greatest security possible. He added several ways to adjust the parameters. In 1949 the device was working properly and several patents were filed.

In 1950, Soviet scientists tested the device to verify its efficiency. Although it worked perfectly, the couple didn't receive the budget needed to continue their research. For ten years, many scientists in the Soviet Union personally experimented with the Kirlian devices, exploring various hypotheses. Whether they were biologists, physiologists, physicists, or physicians, all recognized the value of this invention and the need to subsidize more research. Yet nothing happened until the early sixties. Then a journalist named Ian Belov publicly accused the politic establishment of not supporting this discovery. Money was finally granted to the Kirlians, and the electrophotography process was officially tested in several universities.

In 1968, a long report was written by Viktor Adamenko following the Alma-Ata conference about "biological energy." This report was called "The Biological Essence of the Kirlian Effect." In 1974 Semyon and Valentina Kirlian received the title of "Inventors Decorated with the Order of Merit" from the Praesidium of the Supreme Soviet. Among the collaborators of the Kirlians in the USSR were Viktor Adamenko and V. Inyuchin; they largely contributed to making this process known in the Western world.

However, electrophotography was still relatively unknown until 1968, when two American journalists, Sheila Ostrander and Lynn Schroeder, went to the Soviet Union to attend a congress on extrasensory phenomena. Once they returned to the United States, they wrote a book called *Psychic Discoveries Behind the Iron Curtain*, which was published in 1970. This publication popularized electrophotography. Among other revelations, the book presented photographs of a luminescence emanating from living matter, an aura quickly associated with many different names. In Spiritism it was called *perispirit*, and theosophists and occultists called it *the etheric and auric bodies*. The Russians called it *bioplasma*, von Reichenbach the *odic force*, and Wilhelm Reich *orgone energy*, but it was also known as *bioluminescence*, *mitogenic radiation*, or simply *energy field*.

In the United States of America, Dr. Thelma Moss (a psychologist at the University of California, Los Angeles) discovered the text and the photos. Enthusiastic about these findings, she travelled to the USSR to meet the main researchers. She met a number of them but was not allowed to visit the laboratories. However, she came back with many more documents. Helped by her collaborator, Kendall Johnson, she built a prototype of a low-frequency camera.

In 1978, David Guerdon, a journalist from a short-lived French magazine called *Psi International*, did a very interesting interview of Thelma Moss. A few excerpts are worth translating here:

> In 1968 [said Dr. Thelma Moss], the Kirlians defined the electrophotography that would soon bear their name as: "the conversion of the non-electric properties of the object into electric properties...with a direct transfer of charges from the object to the photographic plate." Their former collaborator Adamenko spoke of a "cold emission of electrons," which can provide unknown information about the nature of organic and inorganic matter. Some wanted to reduce this "cold emission of electrons" to a banal electrical phenomenon, the corona discharge. But, for now, the controversy would take us too far...
>
> I discovered this process quite simply—and like everyone else—by reading the famous book by Ostrander and Schroeder which, in 1970, told us about the prodigious work of Soviet parapsychologists. The authors of this book revealed that an endlessly changing luminescence that emanated from living matter had been photographed. You can imagine my excitement. Had we finally photographed this hypothetical bioenergy?...I wrote to a name mentioned in the bibliography of the book and I was surprised to receive a kind invitation...
>
> Unfortunately, I couldn't see the Kirlians, because they live in a remote area of the USSR in Krasnodar in the Kuban province near the Black Sea, but my trip was nonetheless very successful. I met their collaborator Victor Adamenko in Moscow. Then I went to Siberia, to Alma-Ata, where I was able to speak

with Professor V. I. Iniouchine. Despite his thirty years, he was very knowledgeable. The Soviet authorities did not grant us the right to visit his laboratories, but the professor kindly gave us all his published works and even a diagram of the Kirlian device. I took all this documentation back to the United States. It was these documents that helped us to start our work in our country...

The Kirlian photo is done quite simply, without a camera or lens. All that is required is a source of energy that is placed outside the separated room where the photos are taken. We use a cabin for all our sensory isolation experiences, for example in telepathy. It allows us to get not only darkness, but constant temperature and humidity. A wire connects the power source to a film holder placed on a wooden table. In this frame, we place a photographic film, color or black and white. The object to be photographed is placed directly in contact with the emulsion. For a second, we run an electric current through the object and the film. When it comes to black and white, we work in red light and develop the film immediately. For the color, you need absolute darkness, which creates some problems. To avoid any danger of electric shock, the amperage remains very low (1/10 of a microampere). When we photograph a leaf, we increase the frequency, which increases the intensity of the "aura."

It is important to know that there are now several cameras of different designs around the world. Photos may be different depending on the device, whether they use low or high frequencies, different voltages, sinusoidal or square waves...By changing the frequencies with which we take the photos, we have seen the same object—leaves or fingertips—twinkle in low frequency, changing their shape in a higher one, becoming brighter again at an even higher frequency.

The day when different researchers will decide to compare the results of their experiments, they will first have to standardize their devices (voltage, frequency, waveform, exposure time, etc.).

For example, we move the current from the subject to the film, while the Kirlians do the opposite. And our photos are different.

We are now working on Henry Dakin's device, which gives longer emanations, or on Kendal Johnson's device. We have taken more than ten thousand photos in ten months and our results remain very consistent.

Even if some believe it is something called in physics "the crown effect," we had to prove to them that if indeed it was such a phenomenon, and indeed its existence is indisputable, certain psychic or physiological influences could modify it. It is for this reason that we are developing different hypotheses.

In the same way, several other American researchers, including William Tiller and Stanley Krippner, discovered this photographic process and experimented. In 1972, the first international congress devoted to the human aura outside the Soviet Union was organized in New York.

Over the following years, many conferences were organized on topics related to the human aura or Kirlian photography. In 1978, Dr. Peter Mandel presented his work about the use of Kirlian photography and disease detection. This particular axis was used by various researchers working on therapy.

We should also mention the progress made by Ioan Florin Dumitrescu, as reported by Georges Guilpain in his book on the Kirlian effect. This medical doctor developed a process that would allow this type of photography to be taken without direct contact between the patient and the sensitive plaques, as is the case in the usual process.

There is no doubt that research will continue. Other methods of body and medical photography are used today. Electrophotography has real value, and it broadens horizons far beyond those that researchers suspected. If we consider the traditions and exercises used in this book, such photos match the description of the etheric aura. We hope that more advanced devices will succeed in reaching the level of the astral aura—perhaps even beyond it. Meanwhile, we can use the training provided here to develop our abilities and see for ourselves. If one day we can unite science and psychic abilities, it will greatly benefit both scientists and adepts.

Part Two
EXPERIENCING THE AURA

Chapter Five
SEEING THE AURA—
FIRST STEPS

The second part of this book is a progressive and structured initiation. Every exercise has been designed to be as simple and efficient as possible. I have taught each of the exercises in this book since the '70s up until today, either in public workshops or as part of the Initiatory Orders I am in charge of—they have been tested in a lot of countries. And you are about to follow this amazing path!

Try to follow each of the exercises in this book but, if necessary, remember: you can adapt most of the exercises to your personality, previous experience, and knowledge. Techniques are intended to be assimilated, practiced, and mastered to unveil your true self; this discovery can really change your life and the way you interact with your family and community.

First, you should understand that the ability to see the aura is absolutely natural. For some of us, it happens spontaneously. For others, it can be learned and mastered. Remember that this faculty is within everyone's reach. Starting this training does not require any specific spiritual development.

The perception of the aura can of course be experienced in contact with others, but also with inanimate objects, plants, natural phenomena, or animals. Therefore, we use these elements as topics for the exercises provided in this book.

AN IMPORTANT RECOMMENDATION

I want to draw your attention to a golden rule you must keep in your mind at all times—your mental health is at stake here. Besides serious Initiatory Orders, this is rarely stated in public writings. *Your perception of the astral world and subtle bodies must imperatively remain under your control!* That means that you should only feel or see when you want, and stop when your practice has ended.

You must imagine that the astral vision is used like normal vision: you open your eyes and you see, then you close your eyes and you stop seeing. Nothing should force you to see when you don't want to. Keeping your eyes open all the time could hurt you and eventually deregulate your brain; the same thing occurs with astral vision, and you should be prudent. Do not think that ending your astral vision will diminish your intuition or ability to see the astral world. After all, when you have your eyelids closed, you can still feel or even see a clear light. However, *you* must be the one deciding if you open your eyes or not—nobody else.

The reason for doing this is simple: astral vision implies opening our being to other worlds and kinds of energies. Obviously, they are different than the physical plane. When such opening occurs, we disconnect ourselves from the physical world for a few moments, or at least we move aside the physical realities. We open our spiritual eyes and step into the shining lights of the astral world. When we stop, we are supposed to shut down this vision. If the astral eyes are open at any time and without your consent, little by little you will no longer be able to distinguish the astral world from the physical world. The physical body will constantly be disturbed by feelings, perceptions, and even sounds or visions. Dreams will be affected too because of feelings of presences around the bed. This is how energy work and psychic training, when not well taught, can create disruption in your life.

I am not saying such things lightly. This is important, and I have the duty to warn you. However, if you follow this golden rule and my advice, nothing bad can happen. You will open your soul, see spiritual wonders, and come back to your life in this world. This is the way to safely achieve a real initiation.

THE DIFFERENT TYPES OF VISION

Before we go further, it is important to know that there are three main ways to see the aura and the subtle bodies.

1. The first is to use the physical eyes and make them able to perceive the other reality. In this case, the frontal chakra, sometimes called the "third eye," is activated using the specific position of our eyes. This vision develops as a result of our work with the physical eyes. Consequently, by training our vision, we also increase the energy and the power of our third eye.

2. The second method only uses the third eye. In this case, the physical eyes are unnecessary, and vision is accomplished directly through the frontal chakra. The eyes can be closed, half-closed, or fully opened, for they are not the organs that see. This specific kind of vision can also be used as a way to change the reality that surrounds you. Associated with visualization, these techniques can help you manipulate the energy you are seeing. Human magnetism involves using this faculty, which can have excellent results as long as you know how to train and have enough patience to master it.

3. The third method is mentioned in several religions as *the vision from the soul*. In this case, neither the physical eyes nor the third eye is used. Instead, your whole body opens as a window and your soul, embodied during your life, perceives in a global vision what is around you on the subtle level.

One of these three kinds of vision can be used, or they can occur simultaneously. Your astral vision can also be adapted depending on the various contexts you experience.

USING A NOTEBOOK

It is very useful to get a notebook for writing down your observations. You should create a habit, at least during your time of training, of writing or drawing the results of your experiments and observations. Sketches can be very useful and are more expedient than words.

I strongly recommend taking note of several details that will be useful to you later, when you analyze your progress and your investigations. These details might include the day and time of the experiment, the weather, the lunar phase, the subject observed, the background used, your physical and emotional state, the approximate duration of your observation, and your results (observed and felt). For example:

> May 12, 2016, nice weather, no humidity, waning moon.
>> Observation of a shrub in the park. Clear sky background, very light blue, almost white.
>> I'm a little stressed, but still calm. Duration: fifteen minutes.

RELAXATION

Relaxation is an important step in any psychic training. It allows you to create the perfect state of consciousness to start the practices. Indeed, the concentration required by the exercises and the stress of learning new things can slow down your progress. Starting each practice with relaxation should give you the inner balance that is needed for going further faster and more efficiently.

If you are new to these techniques or are coming back to them, I recommend that you take a few weeks to start practicing deep relaxation. I have recorded a few classes that could help you, but I also want to give you the opportunity to do it on your own.[11] You can read and record the following script and use it in your practices; this is a typical way to practice relaxation or guided meditation. Even if you prefer following the voice of someone else, this process will work. Again, we must emphasize that relaxation is fundamental preparation for any psychic exercise.

General Outline of Relaxation

Initially, you may start by lying flat on the floor. After some practice, you can use a seated posture.

Prior to beginning, arrange your environment so that everything reflects the inner balance you are striving to achieve. Make sure the room is warm

---

11. Naturally, it would be easier to have relaxation exercises conducted by someone who can describe the complete process in the appropriate tone of voice. You can visit my website to find links to recordings that will help you go further.

enough and that your clothes are comfortable and loose. Keep the lighting dimmed and mute any sounds. Stretch out on your back on a firm surface. Let your arms rest on the floor at your sides, loose and relaxed.

Be attentive to your breathing; listen to your breath flow in and out. Watch your chest rise and fall. Remain quiet, breathing gently in and out. Breathe in through your nostrils, not your mouth. Notice the circulation of air through your body as it enters your nostrils, flows into your lungs, and remains there for a while. Notice the flow as you exhale. Relax and quietly enjoy watching this flow. Return to this simple observation from time to time during this exercise.

Now focus your attention on your right foot. Imagine that it is heavy, as if a gentle heat is flooding through it. As soon as you feel this heaviness, imagine it progressively moving up your right leg to your right hip.

Notice your breathing from time to time. Observe the movement of air in and out of your lungs, and then return to the visualization.

Repeat the same process for your left foot and left leg. Notice your breathing again.

Now think about your right hand. Imagine that your hand becomes heavy and that a gentle heat flows down it. Feel your fingers, the top of your hand, the palm of your hand, your wrist, the front of your arm, your right elbow; visualize the heaviness moving up to your right shoulder. Return regularly to the observation of your breathing.

Move the heaviness to your left hand, your left arm, and up to your left shoulder.

Attend to your pelvis, your belly, your back, your chest, and your neck. This visualization, this heat, this heaviness works with your breathing, which you continue to observe from time to time.

Move your attention to your head. Begin with your scalp, the top of your head, and then bring the heaviness and warmth down the nape of your neck toward your back. Feel the heaviness.

Relax your face, beginning with the roots of your hair along your forehead. Move down your face, toward your eyebrows, eyelids, eyes, cheekbones, temples, jaw, and chin. Go down your entire face one more time and end at your neck. Breathe easily and slowly.

Now imagine that your body is heavy without being overly warm. Your entire body enjoys a gentle warmth and torpor. You are entirely relaxed. Observe your breathing and feel this deep, pervasive calm.

Bring the gentle warmth and heaviness to any part of your body that is not yet heavy, warm, and relaxed. Try not to concentrate on any one area for too long, as that will stop the process of the relaxation. It is necessary to act simultaneously as both actor and observer in this process.

Visualize an ovoid of light, a shining mist four inches thick surrounding your whole body. You are at its center. You feel light and relaxed. Observe your breathing and notice how calm and light you feel. As you continue your meditation, the sensations intensify and you feel utterly weightless. Enjoy these sensations deeply without falling asleep. You could also feel like you are swinging in a hammock or floating in comfortably warm salt water. If you have no specific objective while performing this relaxation exercise, it would be helpful at this juncture to visualize a place that you enjoy.

Whether you are lying on the floor or seated in a chair, you may bring yourself back to awareness gradually; it isn't necessary to relax for extended periods. To accelerate the awareness of your physical body, breathe deeply and gently wiggle your toes and fingers. Take your time progressively activating your consciousness and stretching your body. Once you feel fully aware, you may resume your activities.

You should practice this method of relaxation as preparation before any psychic exercise. As we said, it increases your inner potential. When you have practiced the full technique provided several times, you can switch to a shorter version. At that point, I invite you to practice in a seated position. In that event, be seated in a chair when you complete the exercise. At this juncture, you should globalize your relaxation by linking it mentally to a few rounds of breathing cycles, easily connecting the cycles to all the parts of your body. At this level of practice, you can just focus on your breathing and easily reach this level of relaxation.

The faster, seated process will work if you have already integrated the previous one. The efficiency of this practice is founded on the connection between three things: visualization, breathing, and focus. The point is to maintain these three aspects simultaneously during the practice. As you can

imagine, the key is to practice frequently and relentlessly. Repetition is paramount to obtain success.

VISUALIZATION

Strictly speaking, visualization is not required to see the subtle bodies. However, there are two main reasons why you cannot ignore the principles of this
technique: First, visualization focuses the mind. This kind of concentration
is needed in every exercise in this book. Second, visualization is a faculty of
the mind that is used to see the highest planes and bodies. It is fundamental when you are working with your partner without their physical presence,
and in any attempt to practice an out-of-body experience. Creative visualization is a voluntary action aiming for a specific result; it is about creating a
mental image.

It is important to not misunderstand what is meant by the word *visualization*. Most people assume that it is an elaboration of a kind of mental
photography, as if they were looking at a picture. That's not exactly true. You
already know how to make mental pictures, but you generally limit them to
one sense: vision. Of course, some people do not use vision as their main
sense, even if it is generally predominant in today's world. In this regard, it
might be helpful to think about the way a person who was born blind visualizes. Their visual representations would have to be replaced by a combination
of their other perceptions, such as smell, taste, touch, etc.

Understanding this principle should help you recognize how to bring
your imagination under control. The initial step is identical to the act of
thinking about someone or someplace far from you. The subject of your
thoughts must be a person or place you know well. You do this all the time
without any effort. Stop reading for a moment and try it right now—see how
easy it is. If you are at the office or in your living room, think about your
bedroom. Or think about your wife, husband, a friend, a child you love. The
result is immediate. You don't have to do anything special; you have been
doing this all your life.

This is the beginning of taking control over your visualization, which is
the foundation of any psychic development. Remember that this is only the
first step; you haven't actually started to use creative visualization yet. However, becoming aware of this ability is the only way to make progress.

TRAINING AS A COUPLE

Working alone is the easiest way to practice most of the exercises offered in this book. However, you can learn a lot by practicing with a partner. It is important to choose someone you trust and feel comfortable with. During exercises of observation, one is the subject and the other one the observer. In this case, it is essential to switch the roles and compare only after writing down your observations. In other situations, both are working together with the energies or detection of the subtle bodies.

You are not obligated to always work with the same partner. Sometimes it is even more interesting to work with someone else. We have been asked several times if the gender of your partner is important in these practices. The answer is no. Of course, energies can be different, but it only makes the observations more interesting. The only thing we ask is to agree on a common simple principle, which is: *every observation must remain confidential forever*. This relationship of trust is paramount, as not having complete trust can really interfere with the quality of your learning and the results of the observations. This is also something you should apply to everyone else, when you read the auras of strangers.

EXERCISE 1: THE AURA AROUND US

If you've ever seen a crowd from above, you may have seen people who are chatting and keeping a precise distance between each other. You could easily imagine circles surrounding them, as if real invisible walls were protecting them. It can analogically represent the space of freedom necessary for the individual to feel safe. From the subtle energetic standpoint, this behavior can be seen as an involuntary effect of the auric sphere. This is an involuntary perception, as these people are not aware of the process and do not control anything. I invite you to verify this observation yourself. Go outside and look at a crowd from a bridge, for example. Living in Las Vegas gives me a lot of opportunities of this kind.

Such circles change depending on the activity: during a demonstration, at a concert, while walking, etc. Obviously, the kind of energy and its intensity depends directly on the event. It is very helpful to observe these behaviors as often as you can. No need to take notes immediately—you can do that when you return home. Developing this habit of observation is not just a curiosity or leisure; this attitude triggers a reaction in the deepest level of your brain. This process awakes your hidden abilities. After a few weeks or months, almost without noticing it, you should start to feel and see more easily these levels of energy.

After various observations, you can go ahead and start with the direct perception of the subtle bodies. This should start by increasing your awareness of your aura and the people you meet. Here is how you should proceed: When you are in conversation with someone, be aware of the distance between you and them. Obviously, this exercise works even better if you don't know the person you are talking with. It is important to not change your attitude during this observation. Continue your conversation, being aware of this distance. Don't change anything yet—it is important that the person you are talking with does not notice anything. Then, once you are comfortable simultaneously focusing on your awareness and the discussion, start playing with the distance. Move forward very lightly and observe what happens. Then step closer, then farther, then closer, etc. Stop before creating discomfort. Remember to not be too close, as it can be misconstrued. You can also experiment with this process by moving back. No matter which direction you choose, it is important to keep your movement almost imperceptible so you stay the only one aware of it. Notice the unconscious reaction of the person you speak to. They will move without noticing it in an effort to keep their space.

The purpose of these exercises is to show you the presence and effect of the aura. Being aware for short periods of time triggers a reaction in your psyche that helps you develop your ability to perceive and see these levels of energy. You are also building a very important part of the practice, which is to work simultaneously on two levels: the physical one and the energetic one. Strictly speaking, at this stage, it is not about seeing the aura, but rather about being aware of its manifestations and effects. This mental habit is important because one of the fundamental keys of these techniques is to use your visualization.

EXERCISE 2: PERCEPTION OF ATMOSPHERES

In the first exercise, your mission was to be aware of the effects of the aura. That exercise already started to activate your inner ability. In this second practice, you are about to go further by adding a new layer of awareness. The goal is now to feel the presence and nature of the aura.

It is a good idea to link what you are doing in this exercise with the previous one. When you are close to someone, but before you play with the distance between you, be aware of what you feel. This process involves your whole body, not just your mind.

To understand how it works and what you should feel, imagine you are swimming in a warm pool. Then, when you get out, a fresh breeze is blowing. In a second, your whole body will react; this coolness will be a full-body experience. You don't think about it, you just feel it from all the parts of your body. A few seconds after, you will start to think about it and react appropriately, perhaps reaching for a towel. It is the same thing here. You should create the same kind of perception, but instead of the surface of your skin, your aura is the skin that feels and reacts to the other auras. You receive these feelings in your whole body, not just with your intellect.

I invite you to experiment with these perceptions when you speak with someone. You can even transform this perception to achieve a specific goal. For now, play with this awareness and welcome these perceptions. Remember that you are the one in charge—you are starting this process, and you can end it at any time.

You may ask if this perception is identical to the intuition we have when we first meet someone. The answer is yes. The feelings you can have when meeting someone are coming from this contact between the auras. The difference is that this training relies on creating a real awareness and control of the process. This is paramount as you are building your foundations. I cannot emphasize enough the importance of practicing these exercises often.

In my previous explanation, I didn't say anything about the nature of the perception. I am not advising you practice this exercise with any individual. Opening your perception to the subtle energy coming from one's aura is not the same as absorbing the energy, no matter its nature, but before you learn how to build a proper astral filter, you should react accordingly when you feel uncomfortable. The way to do that is to just shut down your feelings, returning to the conversation and your breathing. These two things are enough to achieve disconnection.

After having practiced this exercise a few times, you can work on your perception in various places. To do this, do the same work you just did, but at a specific location. It could be a house, a room, a small public square, or any place that has been inhabited. The specific energy of a place is associated with the memories of the people who lived there, which creates a specific aura and atmosphere you can feel. When you enter a place, pay attention to your spontaneous reactions, your feelings, and your emotions. With time, these perceptions will gradually come faster while being very precise.

THE VISION OF THE AURA

As we mentioned, physical eyes generally do not see subtle energies. Our senses are not all active at the same time; sometimes our perception is relying on several senses, sometimes just one. This is the same for the vision of the aura. In the first two exercises we used a global vision that was not specific to the eyes. The present exercise is starting to use the vision itself, but not the usual one. In chapter 1, we talked about subtle bodies and chakras. The third eye chakra is the location of auric vision, but most of us do not have this chakra already activated. That means we are not spontaneously able to see any level of the subtle bodies. Consequently, we must find a way to activate this frontal chakra through various practices. When the third eye chakra is properly open, we will be able to select the level of subtle energies we want to see.

Activation of the Third Eye

There are two ways to activate this center. The first one is a direct activation using breathing and visualization. The second one is an indirect method that activates this chakra by way of specific practices. These two ways can be used at the same time. As you continue to use the third eye and develop your psychic muscles, you can increase the potential of the center; obviously, this is not the same thing as focusing on it. This section will discuss the activation and strengthening of the third eye.

First Stage

As with each training described in this book, this activation is simple to practice. The difficult aspect is to be consistent in your training for a significant duration. We cannot achieve something in a few days, but in weeks and months we can. Keep in mind that even if parts of this process can be found in religious practices, no faith is required to succeed in your practice. Aspects of this process are also used in yoga, sometimes associated with asanas. Don't worry—you are doing a psychic training. Even if such association is possible, it is not required.

Twice a day, sit in whatever position is comfortable for you. Keep your back straight, align your spine, and slightly extend your head to the sky by raising the back of your skull. Relax your shoulders. If you are sitting on a chair, keep your legs parallel, your feet on the floor, and the palms of your hands either on the arms of the chair or on your thighs.

Start to observe your breathing and relax. Follow the movement of your chest. Feel the air moving in and moving out. Continue this process for a few minutes, just following this harmonious movement without any mental representation. Enjoy this flow.

Then, turn your attention to the center of your forehead. Focus on a spot that is one inch beneath your skull. Do not do anything besides keeping your focus on this point. During this process several things may occur, but two are the most frequent. First, your physical eyes could move as if they are trying to see this point. This creates a tension that could cause a headache. Second, a tension can develop in the center of your forehead with the same possible outcome. To avoid this, you should do several things simultaneously: while you continue breathing, relax the muscles of your face, your jaw, your cheekbones, the eye sockets, your eyelids, the muscles of your eyes, and eventually the muscles of your forehead. Remember that you should relax those muscles without losing your focus on the spot. Again, breathing will help you achieve this step.

Keep your focus. At this stage, you are not gazing at something specific. You are just breathing, focusing on this dot, and relaxing your face and upper body. That's all. Continue to breathe and keep your focus.

Do this for three to five minutes to start, twice a day, usually in the morning and evening. When you feel you have mastered this inner work of staying relaxed, add a few very short periods (a few seconds) during the day, no matter where you are or the position you're in. Close your eyes, place your focus for a few seconds, release, and open your eyes. This acts as a reactivation and continuation of the work you are doing twice a day.

SECOND STAGE

There is another stage that can help you in the more advanced techniques of astral vision. You can start the second stage once you have mastered the process of focus I just explained. This second stage is simple to describe but takes a little while to control.

The goal is to proceed in the same way, but with your physical eyes open. Look normally around you, without interrupting what you are doing, but place your focus on the center of your forehead. Remember to be relaxed. If there are people around you, they shouldn't notice anything.

Even though this technique is essential, you should limit the number of times you practice a day, as well as the duration. If your focus is fast and efficient, two or three practices during the day for thirty seconds to one minute are enough. This exercise also works as a warm up when you are reading auras.

As you can see, the goal is to awaken and activate your third eye. This is not the astral vision itself, but it is what you need to succeed and master this ability.

———

Now it is time to take things a step further. We are going start to use our physical gaze to see another level of reality. As you can imagine, there is a long way to go between first sight and having full control. This is different for everyone. However, don't worry too much, as the first perceptions are relatively easy and quick to obtain.

EXERCISE 3: VISION OF PRANA

It is relatively easy to feel and see the prana that is carried in the air around us. As I have explained, the density of prana can change a lot, depending on the location and weather. One of the best and easiest ways to start is to use the blue sky as a background. This will be a very enjoyable experience.

When the weather is good, go outside. Find a place where you can easily see the sky and stretch out on the ground or on a lounge chair. Lie comfortably, almost horizontally, facing the sky. Start to relax and breathe regularly. It is important to relax your face and also your whole body.

You should do this exercise when the sun is not high in the sky, or at least not in your field of vision. If the light is intense, slightly close your eyelids, but try to not have your eyelashes obstructing your vision—the goal is to reduce the brightness received by your eyes. Don't try to see anything yet. Just submerge into that blue depth you are looking at.

This sensation appears easily if you do not have anything in your field of vision but the blue sky. Tree branches, for example, could interfere negatively. Look deep in the blue sky and feel that you are moving in that direction, or even diving into it. It is good to feel that, but today we are not doing an out-of-body experience, so don't drift too far into that sensation. Keep your focus.

Once you are relaxed, you have the role of the observer. First, observe the different particles that move in front of your eyes. There are different filaments, spheres, and all kinds of shapes. They can have a very light color, but most of the time they are almost transparent. These small particles are usually impurities on the surface of your eye; the blue background of the sky reveals the presence of these particles. To clearly identify them and to be sure, try to blink or move your eyes slowly. The particles move and return to their previous place. When you are fully aware of this physical level, look further into the deep blue sky. You should see something you have already spotted, which are small, transparent spheres. They look like tiny bubbles, apparently moving randomly. They seem to be flying in a light wind, sometimes in large concentrations, sometimes smaller. Near highly ionized places, you should see a higher number of spheres. These tiny spheres are the components of prana you can perceive at this stage of your training. Waterfalls, mountain streams, breaking ocean waves, water jets, and mountain peaks are the best places to observe a high concentration of prana.

It is important to practice this exercise. It doesn't require a lot of effort, it allows you to enjoy the wonders of nature, and its effects are paramount. This seemingly simple exercise has long-lasting effects on your inner abilities! You can achieve good success without a lot of effort, which is great. The surface of the sky and the vibratory presence of prana facilitate the natural process of this very special kind of vision.

Chapter Six
SEEING THE ENERGY BODY

In the '80s, computer-generated illustrations were created. They were called *autostereograms*. In this technique, a repetitive pattern of mosaics is hiding a 3D illustration different than the apparent and immediately visible pattern. To discover this hidden illustration, it is necessary to focus your eyes as if you were looking at a faraway point. This technique is called *diverging your eyes*, *stereopsis*, or *stereo vision*.

You can apply the same technique of vision to see the etheric body. The etheric body is the denser part of your aura that reflects the energy of your physical body—consequently, this is the easiest one to see. To achieve this perception, begin by relaxing your whole face. Start with a short focus on your third eye, then place your gaze as you did for the vision of prana in the blue sky (see chapter 5). At all times, your vision should be clear. If it becomes blurry, come back to your focus.

To see the etheric, you must place your gaze a specific way. Usually, to see something you have to focus on it: both eyes are converging on what you are looking at. But here, you are going to look at an object, a plant, your hands, or another individual by keeping the focus of your eyes on both sides of it. The left is looking on the left side and the right on the right side. The axes of vision of your two eyes are therefore somewhat parallel. This gives a stability to your gaze that you should maintain without tension, and without blurring the subject of your vision.

When your focus is placed far away from the subject in front of you, after a few seconds you should see the luminous halo of the etheric a few inches over the body. The usual first reaction is to focus on this luminous halo, but if you do that, the halo immediately disappears and you will return to the vision of the physical level.

———————

In one of the workshops my wife, Patricia, and I organized, a student described this phenomenon very well while observing a plant: "At first, it was difficult to see this etheric field. It was appearing and disappearing for no reason, even without blinking my eyes. Then it stabilized. It was quite thick. But as soon as I was looking at it, it was disappearing again. When I stopped my temptation to focus on it, the vision stabilized. Its color was blue gray and appeared to be full of small silver bubbles. As I continued to observe, I could see thin rays of light, like filaments radiating from the plant and creating this etheric. The limit was not very clear as these rays were vanishing in the air, their density diminishing with distance. Having this vision gave me sensations of power, energy, and peace."

So be careful when you begin to see the etheric. Do not change the position of your gaze. We could say that you see it "out of the corner of your eye." You must be able to look without fixing your gaze. Train yourself. At first you will only see a smokelike haze, but eventually a few colors can be seen. Do not try to speed up the process. Just relax and observe what is happening. Carefully follow the technique I just explained. You will be amazed how easy it is to see the etheric. As soon as you understand how to place your gaze, the vision occurs!

This technique is the first key to the practice that will lead you to mastering this art. Like everything else, it is the know-how that makes the difference, and it can only be acquired through experience and will.

SOME ADVICE AT THIS STAGE

During the first part of your training, it is better to not take notes during your observations. Taking notes could interrupt the still-fragile connection with astral reality. You could have trouble coming back to the observation and rapidly refocusing. It takes time to do that easily, but working with autostereograms can help you. Eventually, the time will come when you realize that taking notes does not interrupt your observations.

To make the task easier, you can take notes on illustrations. It is easier to take notes on a representation rather than writing a detailed description. You can draw your own outline of the human body, or search for an image online and print it out.

We also recommend that you try to not be disturbed during these exercises. If you are at home, do not hesitate to mute your phone and move it away from you. Some prefer to practice these exercises at a time of day when they are sure not to be interrupted, whether it is late evening or very early morning. Do what you think is most appropriate to find a moment that favors concentration and relaxation.

VISION OF THE ETHERIC

The vision of the etheric is the first step that will lead you to the perception of the human aura. This aspect is often overlooked by students in an immediate attempt to perceive the aura and the shimmer of its colorful lights. But, like a beginner who wants to climb a steep cliff without any training, this is undoubtedly a real challenge and a very dangerous thing to do. The best way to start any training is by building the foundation, which is often made of very simple steps. Then, while mastering these practices, our capacity increases, often without us even noticing! It is for this reason Patricia and I are very careful with the details of the exercises and why we find it necessary to explain the risks—doing so keeps this process under your control.

Many writings about astral vision give good advice and explanations, but they are fragmented and usually do not offer a full and progressive method such as this one. Trying to immediately observe the highest level of the aura is like looking directly at the sun without any protection. It can be difficult, painful, and deeply disturbing. You can hurt yourself and create illusions that are disruptive, eventually slowing down and weakening your progress. It is important to emphasize that we strongly believe that it is better to follow a natural and progressive training. It is necessary to create trust in your abilities and let them emerge from the deepest part of your being. It is for this reason that the etheric exercises in this book are so detailed. Then it will be easier for you to transition to the whole perception of the subtle bodies. It is essential to consider our deep and hidden psychological obstacles so we can bypass them to obtain rapid and good results. This is what I prepared for you here.

I strongly suggest practicing seeing the etheric a few times before diving into the rest of this chapter. The exercises that follow are intended to gradually help you master this perception. Some of them are intended to be practiced with external elements, such as stones, plants, or animals. Others can be placed in the category of "know yourself" by looking at your own etheric. Working in pairs helps you go even further, observing your partner and eventually everyone else. In the exercises, we always describe what you should do, but this is an ideal outcome of the practice—it is not always possible to reach this goal. Adapt if necessary, and come as close as possible to the exercise's goal.

EXERCISE 4: THE ETHERIC BODIES OF OBJECTS AND MINERALS

Everything around you has an etheric body, and even sometimes an aura. Any object has a memory, a kind of recording of everything that has happened to this object. All of this creates an energy charge that creates a subtle body somewhat like ours. Consequently, it is possible to observe this etheric and, eventually, explore the past of this object.

When you observe an object, visions from its past might emerge; if this is the case, just notice it and let them go away. That is not our focus today—we are only focusing on the manifestation of the object's aura.

FIRST STEP: NEAR YOU

Scan everything around you. Choose any object that attracts your attention at this very moment. It could be something you're wearing, such as a bracelet, watch, ring, or pendant. If the object is small, raise it so that it is not directly on a table, but as if suspended in the air. Suspend it at the height of your eyes when you are seated. Place your notebook and a pen, coloring pencils, or markers in front of you.

1. Start with the relaxation and breathing techniques in chapter 5.
2. Once the relaxation process is complete, draw the outline of the chosen object in your notebook. (We recommend drawing in black ink.)

3. While maintaining deep and balanced breathing, start to place your stereo vision, gazing in the direction of the object. Your shoulders should still be relaxed, with the palms of your hands resting on your thighs. Keep your focus, avoiding tension in your face and eyes. After a few seconds or minutes, you should see a halo emerging around the object. Keep the awareness of this manifestation and start to analyze it: notice its thickness, density, luminosity, and color.

4. Record the details of your observations in your notebook. Add any remarks as necessary. If you forget something, return to the astral vision and then write down any new information you think could be useful.

5. Once the drawing of the etheric is complete, pay attention to the possible colors that could begin to appear. Be aware that at first you might feel colors more than you actually see them. At this stage, the colors are not stable, so you could almost consider this manifestation of colors as a mirage. Don't be troubled by this instability; it is a normal process. Record the colors when you see or feel them. These colors will become gradually clearer and last longer. We can compare these colors to light waves that move in the etheric.

6. Record everything and trust yourself. When you think that everything has been recorded, you can end the practice.

7. Close your eyes and relax for a few moments, breathing deeply and regularly. Focus on your breathing and do not think about the observations you just did. When you feel relaxed, open your eyes.

8. Review your notes. If necessary, reorganize a few things to clarify what you wrote or drew.

SECOND STEP: COLORED CHALK STICKS

When I started to organize trainings, I used colored chalk sticks as subjects of observation. This step forward is important because it will help you compare the subtle energy of elements that are different only in color. Before you proceed, choose three different-colored chalk sticks.

Take one of the chalk sticks and place it in front of you at the height of your eyes. Use the same process as in the first step of the exercise. Observe the chalk, then record your observations. Switch to the next chalk stick and do the same. After doing the observation on the third chalk stick, end your practice as usual.

You can proceed in the same way with colored candles, but do not light them. Observation of the flame is not a practice you should do at this stage.

THIRD STEP: METALS

After training with colors, it is useful to experiment with different materials. Traditionally, for this step, you should observe three metals: gold, silver, and a permanent magnet.

Repeat the same observation process as you did previously; you should now be very familiar with the process. Record the differences between each type of metal. Do not be disturbed by the possible differences in the shapes. Instead, focus on the essence of the energetic field surrounding the objects.

FOURTH STEP: ROCKS, PRECIOUS STONES, AND CRYSTALS

When we talk about stones, we are moving closer to living organisms. It is a common attitude to consider stones inert, without any kind of consciousness—they are not really moving in front of us, so we conclude they are not living. But anyone who has meditated on mountains or rocky rivers, for example, knows that something powerful is hidden in the rocks. Consciousness exists, but not in the same way as ours. The pace of time is different.

Shamanism can give us a similar experience. I remember meditating on a flat rock of granite near the top of a mountain. Clouds were low in the valley. The air was pure and charged with particles of energy carried by the humidity. The rock was quite cold and a little humid. Moss was visible on this rock. Only clouds were slowly moving toward me, surrounding me from time to time in a kind a ghostly mist. During this long meditation, while practicing specific breathing techniques, my subtle body began to descend into the rock. Progressively I felt the consciousness of the rock. It was living, but at a very different pace. It was a kind of watcher. Civilizations were rising and falling, battles were fought, and everything around was moving and vanishing. The rock was there, watching, moving, and thinking throughout it all, but at a different pace. Its memory was huge and impressive. Compared to it, we were like mayflies, nothing more. Smaller rocks are like that in a way. We can communicate with them. We can feel and see their subtle bodies.

Next time you go for a walk outside, choose a rock. Any kind of rock works, but choose one that attracts you for some reason. Avoid any conceptualization, symbolic connections, etc.; just choose a random rock you like. (At this stage, avoid choosing a specific crystal like those sold in stores.) Try to choose the rock from a place where it would not have been directly touched by anyone for a long time, perhaps never. After you've chosen your rock, place it in a clean tissue and do not let anyone else touch it.

Then you should proceed as you did previously for the observation of the etheric body, either outdoors or indoors. It is a good idea to collect more than one stone so you can compare their invisible bodies as you did with the chalk sticks.

Continue this exploration with precious stones and crystals. You should proceed in the same way you did in the previous exercise. Try to avoid any choice dictated by anything other than your own free will and intuition. The nature and density of the etheric bodies of precious stones and crystals is quite peculiar and interesting. As such, it will be a good training for you.

These gradual and simple exercises will help you develop your clairvoyance along with relaxation and breathing. Gradually, you should also discover better self-confidence, which allows you to explore the realms around you more deeply.

EXERCISE 5: THE PLANT KINGDOM

By now, you might have realized that these trainings are going through each kingdom. We are now about to take a step forward by observing plants. Here is a helpful tip: it is easiest to observe plants in containers, as you can place them in front of an appropriate background.

Proceed in the same way you already did for the previous subjects. However, in this case, we encourage you to make several observations of the same plant at different times of the day and in various types of weather. Every time you practice, remember to record the variety of plant, the time, and the weather. This will be important when you compare your observations. It is interesting to observe different types of plants, such as succulents, cacti, or flowers. They will have different etheric bodies.

After you are satisfied with your work, you are going to take another step forward.

1. Choose two plants and place them a short distance from each other. Observe the etheric bodies and record.

2. Move the plants closer and observe the possible differences, then move them farther away from each other and do the same.

3. Change plants and repeat your experiment.

This is the first time you are using two elements, one with the other. If you are curious, you can extend this experiment by repeating the same steps with two stones.

WILD PLANTS

You can now start to practice outside, in a forest or a park. Choose, for example, a tree. Sit down to observe it. The best background for your observation is a clear and blue sky. In this situation, the etheric body will be easily visible. It would be best if the light source is located on the side, so light is not facing you or behind you.

1. After choosing your tree and a good location, sit as comfortably as possible.

2. Relax for a few moments, calming your breath. If you wish, you can lie down—just make sure you can still see the tree and the blue background.

3. Slightly squint your eyes without closing them. Continue to breathe deeply and regularly. Relax as you begin to see the etheric body of the tree.

4. When you see it, look around the foliage with your eyes, then come back to the starting point and pay attention to the width of the etheric. Do you perceive filaments of light, colors, or movements of the light? Do you see the pranic exchanges?

5. Blink your eyes to end the perception, then relax. Come back to the sensation of your body and the place you are sitting or lying.

6. Write down what you saw, if you didn't record anything during the observation.

We used the example of the tree because it is a very powerful creature, but we advise you to continue your observations on different varieties of plants, such as shrubs, bonsai, or plants that grow in your garden. You may find it helpful to place the plant you're observing in front of a neutral background, whether it is the sky or a large piece of cardboard. With time, this won't be necessary.

We also recommend observing the same plant at different times of the day or in different weather: a beautiful sunny day, before a thunderstorm, after the rain, etc. You should always record the results of your observations.

EXERCISE 6: THE ANIMAL KINGDOM

If you have pets, they can be interesting subjects to watch. The same is true of other animals that you might observe around you. The technique to see the etheric bodies of animals is similar to what you have already practiced. The challenges here are the absence of a carefully chosen background as well as the movements of the animal. It is important to place your stereo vision quickly and to keep it as long as possible while the animal is moving. For this reason, we recommend starting with static animals that are quietly sleeping.

A fascinating experiment is to observe the etheric body before an animal eats in the morning or after a walk. Then do the same one hour afterward. Notice the difference.

Multiply the experiences and subjects to measure the differences.

EXERCISE 7: YOUR ETHERIC HAND

It is now time to reach the upper level of training and to transition to human observation. You should start with yourself, then with a partner, and eventually will be able to work with others.

1. As you did for your previous observations, choose a clear background, such as a large sheet or just the wall of the room. Usually, we recommend a white or cream background, but we've discovered that we can also obtain very good results using a black or dark background. Consequently, it is a good idea for you to try both and see which one works the best for you. This background should be on a wall, on a table, or wherever it is convenient to place your hand between this screen and

your eyes. Choose a background large enough to cover the surface of your hand plus at least six inches (fifteen centimeters) on each side.

2. Ideally, the light should be indirect or located to the side so that the light is not coming from in front of you or behind you.

3. Sit back and relax for a few moments, following the sequences we explained in chapter 5.

4. Extend your arm in front of you. The back of your hand should be visible, as if you are going to place your hand on the surface you chose. Breathe deeply and regularly.

5. Then place your gaze. You should see the etheric light surrounding your hand. Carefully follow our previous recommendations. Seeing the first perception can take from a few seconds to a few minutes. If for some reason you cannot see the etheric light after four or five minutes, which is very rare, stop and come back to it later. Remember that it is better to have short, regular training than to practice just once for a long time.

6. When you see this luminosity, slightly move your gaze around the edge of the hand to perceive the differences in thickness, density, or brightness, mainly at the fingertips.

7. When you start to see all of this, focus a little more to see as many details as possible. This will increase your potential.

8. Then, release your position and stop this exercise. Write any observations in your notebook.

EXERCISE 8: CIRCULATION OF ENERGY

This exercise builds on exercise 7.

INDIVIDUAL PROCESS

1. As you did for your previous observations, choose a clear background, such as a large sheet or just the wall of the room. Use a white or cream background, or a black or dark background if that works better for you. This background should be on a wall, on a table, or wherever it is convenient to place your hand between this screen and your eyes.

Choose a background large enough to cover the surface of your hand plus at least six inches (fifteen centimeters) on each side.

2. Ideally, the light should be indirect or located to the side so that the light is not coming from in front of you or behind you.

3. Sit back and relax for a few moments, following the sequences we explained in chapter 5.

4. Extend both arms out in front of you with the backs of your hands facing you as if you were going to place your hands on the background. Move the hands so that the tips of the fingers are facing each other about three inches (eight centimeters) apart. Breathe deeply and regularly.

5. Place your gaze in the usual way to perceive the etheric glow.

6. Once you see this beautiful luminous halo, focus on the tips of the fingers of both hands. The energy is usually extending from one hand to the other. Observe and analyze what is happening. Try to observe more carefully: Is there a direction to the flow of energy? Is there a difference in color from one hand to the other?

7. Then keeping your vision, slowly move your hands closer to each other, and after few seconds, move them farther apart. See what is happening. Is there a modification of the color, the flow, or the density? Also notice your sensations.

8. When you start to see all of this, focus a little more to see as many details as possible. This will increase your potential.

9. Then, release your position and stop this exercise. Write any observations in your notebook.

Obviously, your observations will vary according to your physical state, the kind of food you ate in the previous hours, your environment, and many other factors. Everything is an opportunity to experiment more and learn. If, for example, you just drank alcohol and then observed your etheric, the light would be more diffuse, less bright and sharp, than usual. It is as if the light is transformed into a slightly illuminated fog. This change is even more obvious if you observe the etheric body of someone who is an alcoholic.

Also compare the quality of your etheric body after taking a walk or going for a hike. To the same effect, observe the etheric after swimming in a river or the sea. In these cases, the light is usually brighter, and the rays between your hands will extend further.

TWO-PERSON PROCESS

Patricia and I love teaching this practice during workshops we organize. It is important to remember that working in a two-person team creates an exchange of energy called *animal magnetism* or *mesmerism*. Working with a partner involves the energy of each of you.

1. Find a partner. Each of you should sit on a cushion placed on the floor, facing each other. The purpose of this practice is the vision of a subtle body. If the floor is not dark enough or has a pattern that could disrupt your vision, place a dark piece of cardboard on the floor between you and your partner.

2. Proceed to your relaxation and breathing. Keep your eyes closed. Feel the energy around you.

3. Extend both arms, palms down, placing the tip of your fingers in front of the tip of the fingers of your partner. Your fingertips should be approximately three or four inches apart. In this position, you should see the hands from above. Observe in silence.

4. Once you and your partner see the light of the etheric bodies, move your hands closer, then move them away. Every movement should be smooth and slow.

5. The energy flows differently according to the hands you choose. Consequently, try to cross the arms. Have your right hand facing your partner's right hand, and vice versa. Observe any differences, not just in the vision, but also in whatever sensations you notice.

6. Release your position and stop the exercise. Record any observations in your notebook.

EXERCISE 9: THE ETHERIC BODY AROUND THE HEAD

At this stage of your training, you could have the desire to go faster and see the whole etheric body. However, let's take a moment to consider a very powerful and energetic part of the body: the head. First, it is good to know that it is more difficult to see the whole head's etheric body than to see part of it.

Second, the head's etheric body is easier to see than other areas of the body, and this is for many reasons. Among them, the activity of the brain generates electricity and energy; the head contains powerful chakras; the head has a connection with higher levels of energy; and the head is often unclothed. When hairs are present, they reinforce this magnetic field.

INDIVIDUAL PROCESS

The main difference between this exercise and the previous exercises is that you cannot directly observe your head. So, you need to use a mirror.

1. Sit in front of a mirror. Place it far enough away that you can see the totality of your head in the reflection, as well as enough space around it to see the etheric light.

2. Ideally, the light should be indirect or located to the side so that the light is not coming from in front of you or behind you.

3. Sit back and relax for a few moments, following the sequences we explained in chapter 5.

4. As the head is larger than your hand, remember the way you looked at pets or plants. Your vision should embrace your whole head at once for the etheric body to become visible. Remember that at this stage, you can see this light on the sides of the head. Your eyes should be placed as usual to obtain this specific vision.

5. When you see the light, observe any details that seem useful to you, as you did for your hand. Use your previous training to see if there is any effect on the energy: Focus on your third eye and observe the effects. Keep the focus for a while and see what is happening. Usually, the density and thickness of the etheric are amplified. It is also interesting to practice this vision at different times of the day or in different moods.

6. Release your position and stop the exercise. Remember to record everything in your notebook, including the external circumstances and time.

TWO-PERSON PROCESS

During partnered exercises of observation, one is the subject and the other the observer. In this case, it is essential to switch the roles and compare only after the records. In other situations, both are working together with the energies or detection of the subtle bodies.

1. For this practice, sit on a cushion on the floor or in a chair. Your partner should stand three feet (one meter) in front of the chosen background (a wall, for example). The distance between the two of you should be between six and nine feet (two to three meters). You can change these distances as needed.

2. Ideally, the light should be indirect or located to the side so that the light is not coming from in front of you or behind you.

3. Sit back and relax for a few moments, following the sequences we explained in chapter 5.

4. Place your gaze and start to observe the etheric light of your partner's head. Your vision should embrace your partner's whole head at once for the etheric body to become visible. Remember that at this stage, you can see this light on the sides of the head. If you are able to keep the vision while recording your observations in your notebook, please do so.

5. Try to see if there are differences in the density of the etheric in different parts of the head. Do you see a variation in the thickness and brightness on the sides, on the top, or behind the head? You can ask your subject to turn their head, if necessary, so that you can see it from the front and then from the side.

6. After a while, inform your partner that the observation has been completed. End the exercise and record your observations if you haven't already. Then, switch roles so that your partner becomes the observer.

It is a good idea to improve your understanding of this subtle body by doing these observations at different times of the day and with various individuals. If you are working with the same partner, which is fine, try to do it when the situation is different. For example, observe after having a drink, after eating dinner, before and after a walk, etc. If one of you has a headache, see or feel what is different. In these cases, you do not have to formally follow the whole process—just sit close by and observe.

There are a lot of opportunities to learn. Don't miss an opportunity to exercise your new talent, wherever you are.

EXERCISE 10: YOUR WHOLE ETHERIC BODY

Now is the time to go big and observe your whole etheric body in a more comprehensive way. The best way to practice is by starting on yourself. We recommend using a large standing floor mirror, but you could also use a wall mirror as long as it allows you to observe the upper part of your body, from the hips to the head.

INDIVIDUAL PROCESS

We recommend wearing light, comfortable clothes that are not too tight. Avoid any tension on your skin as much as possible. Wear something you like that keeps your body at the perfect temperature so you feel relaxed. It is best to choose a natural fabric such as cotton or linen, and to choose fabric that is a solid color. It should be perfectly clean when you start this exercise. If you are comfortable with it and the temperature allows it, it would be ideal to be naked. In that case, nothing would interfere with your perception.

1. Sit on a chair or a stool. You should be about seven feet (two meters) away from the mirror so that you can see your body and space around you. It is perfectly fine to only see your upper body.

2. Ideally, the light should be indirect or located to the side so that the light is not coming from in front of you or behind you.

3. Sit back and relax for a few moments, following the sequences we explained in chapter 5.

4. At first, your observations should focus on the periphery of your body. Try not trying to see specific colors at the beginning. Instead, pay attention to the etheric body's density and thickness.

5. When your vision is stable, try to be more attentive to tiny details such as modification of density in some parts, lighter or darker zones, rays of light, empty space, significant differences of thickness, etc. If there is a lot to notice, you can immediately record a few important observations in your notebook.

6. The etheric body is quite easy to observe around your body. However, you know that it is present all around you. Chakras and other channels are mainly located in front of you. Now is the time to transition to a different kind of vision, or, more specifically, to extend your vision to what is in front of your body. You can do that by activating your third eye, as you did in the first trainings. Keeping your stereo vision and the perception of the luminous zone around you, be aware of your third eye. If you properly did the training on the third eye, you should immediately feel its presence and activation. It is like a pressure on your forehead. After a few seconds, you should also feel this part of your body slightly warming. Continue to look with your physical eyes. You can now associate both sensations: the vision of your eyes and the vision by the third eye. You are seeing this invisible body in front of your physical body. This is not like the vision on the edge of the physical body, but a different kind of vision that is more interior. It is as if you see this subtle body without using the physical vision. This is the moment in your training when you will simultaneously use the two different kinds of vision. For your brain, it will be the same, and both visions will be merged. Take the time to familiarize yourself with this specific kind of perception.

7. After practicing this exercise several times, you could notice various colors appearing on this body. You can record these colors, but do not focus too much on what is manifested right now; we are working on a specific level of energy, and colors are very limited. The colors you are starting to notice are coming from higher levels of energy. To avoid any confusion, it is best to notice the colors and let them go. If colors do manifest, this is a good sign of your progress.

8. When you are again aware of your surroundings, you can end the exercise and fully come back to the material world.

9. It is a good idea to record what you remember and maybe to correct a few things you wrote during the observation. Drawings are welcome; they can help you specify locations in the subtle body.

It is very useful to repeat this exercise several times and notice any changes that occur. These observations will help you understand the interactions between your life, your environment, and your energetic body. If you chose to wear clothes, try this exercise naked sometime. Notice the difference. Can you see more clearly, or less? Are you feeling more comfortable because you are focusing on a higher level of consciousness and energy? Everything is important in this observation. You can also try to see the etheric of the clothes you wore during the day. Remember that everything keeps a memory of what is happening; this is the case for you, for objects, and for your clothes. So, using different clothes during your observations could change the perception and the light that surrounds you. As we have said several times, everything is important, and it is best to keep your curiosity active.

This technique is something you can use a lot in the next exercises on the aura. You will need to practice this exercise several times to master it. Don't worry, this is normal, and you will progress faster than you think.

TWO-PERSON PROCESS

This process is similar to exercise 9, when you observed the etheric body around your partner's head. The only difference now is that you should explore the whole body of your partner, or at least the upper body.

1. For this practice, sit on a cushion on the floor or in a chair. Your partner should stand three feet (one meter) in front of the chosen background (a wall, for example). The distance between the two of you should be between six and nine feet (two to three meters). You can change these distances as needed.

2. Ideally, the light should be indirect or located to the side so that the light is not coming from in front of you or behind you.

3. Sit back and relax for a few moments, following the sequences we explained in chapter 5. At first, it is better not to visualize anything. To avoid any thoughts that can modify the observation, it is best to close your eyes and focus on your breathing, noticing the air coming in and going out.

4. When you are ready, place your vision in the usual way to look at your partner's etheric body. Your first perception should be peripheric, trying to avoid focusing on one specific part of the body.

5. Once the first examination has been done, go further in your observation. Find the details of this energetic body: thickness, density, radiance, possible colors, particular manifestations, etc.

6. It is important to keep your focus. For that, you need to limit the duration of the practice. At this point, such observation should not exceed five minutes.

7. End your vision with a few breaths. When you feel good and rooted, scan the place you are in with each of your physical senses. Open your eyes if they are half-closed. Tell your partner the examination is over.

8. Record your observations if you haven't already. Then, switch roles so that your partner becomes the observer. It is best to wait to compare experiences until both of you have completed the exercise.

After having performed this exercise a few times, you can start to use your concentration and visualization to move your energy. The observer should be able to witness this movement. Suppose, for example, the subject maintains awareness of the breath while focusing on the left shoulder. Such concentration for a few minutes increases the blood flow in this part of the physical body. It will also activate the energy. Consequently, that area of the etheric body will change. This modification occurs in different ways, depending on the person. It is a very useful training for both parties, both to learn how to direct inner energy to a specific location and to notice the modifications. This is a very dynamic exercise that Patricia and I use a lot during our workshops.

EXERCISE 11: THE ETHERIC BODIES

This exercise is crucial, and it is important to carefully follow the steps explained here.

By now, you should be able to see the etheric body faster, and you should be more confident in your abilities. It is good to exercise your new talent in your daily life. Any situation can work, but the conditions we recommend are as follows: Try to find a public place, a terrace at a café or restaurant, a park, a square, or a beach. Obviously, you need people you can observe. We recommend being discreet when you observe individuals not aware of your presence.

You should be approximately thirty to sixty feet (ten to twenty meters) away from the person you are observing. Your attitude is important—do not stare at others in a way that could be seen as intrusive, embarrassing, or even aggressive. If you do, the exercise could end in a confusing way. Find a way to be discreet. Pretend to be busy reading a book, using an electronic device, or drinking something.

All the usual observation steps should be carried out in a discreet manner.

1. Start with a few breaths to relax and enjoy the moment. It is recommended to increase your awareness of the place and of your position by using all your senses one by one. You should reach progressively a real state of mindfulness.

2. Pay attention to people walking around, but without trying to see anything specific. Keep your relaxation. Be curious about everything that is going on, but without focusing your gaze.

3. Then, after a while, choose someone who is standing or seated at the right distance. Keeping in mind the recommendations about discretion, change your vision to see their etheric body. Usually, you can notice a kind of void that is whitish-gray very quickly. For now, don't try to see more than that; just notice this light and move your focus to someone else. Notice any differences.

4. Once you have done this successfully, do the same type of observation to people walking. It is best to focus on individuals who are walking slowly. Observe what happens to the etheric body when they move.

5. This is a dynamic practice, so return your focus to someone who is seated. Try to go further in your observation and see details of this energetic body: thickness, density, radiance, colors, etc.

6. At this stage, do not continue your observations for too long, as your focus could decrease. Try to keep your curiosity and excitement. This is one of the keys to your success. It is important to limit the duration of this exercise to a maximum of fifteen minutes.

7. End the exercise with a few breaths and relaxing your mind and body. Close your eyes, keeping your breathing calm and regular. If you have any thoughts, let them go where they want, but do not focus on one

in particular. When you feel good and rooted, scan the place you are in with each of your physical senses. Open your eyes if they are half-closed.

8. Complete your notes if necessary, then return to your daily life. If you'd like, you can repeat this exercise after pausing for at least thirty minutes.

———

At this stage, we can assume you have mastered the vision of the etheric body, although it is up to you to go further and further into the precise analysis of it. You should use the previous chapters to analyze your findings. It is essential to remind you that such vision can be used on many levels. This is a good way to find diseases even before they exist in the physical body.

You are now ready to go forward and develop your astral vision even more by starting to see the astral aura. Even if you saw colors in the etheric body, they manifest at its upper limit and are part of the astral body. The development of your vision is in process, and the only thing to do is to extend this ability.

We are following a didactic method that is building your foundations while avoiding illusions. Everything we have done so far is with that in mind. Remember that the astral world is a place of wonders, but it can also be a space of delusion. You better be well prepared!

Chapter Seven
SEEING THE AURA

What we usually call the aura is an invisible body linked to the astral world. The vision of this "astral aura" involves two different levels of perception. It is important to explain in detail what they are, to understand how they work and how it is possible to switch from one to the other. There are two methods of perception: either by developing your physical vision even more, or by relying directly on the third eye, without using your physical eyes. In almost all the previous exercises, you used your physical eyes to observe the etheric body. You have increased your eyes' natural capacities to give them the ability to see what is invisible for most other people. In some exercises, you activated your third eye to start to transition to another kind of vision. As surprising as it may seem, your third eye can observe the aura, and even higher levels of energy, with great accuracy.

Let us consider the first method of perception, in which we observe the world with our physical eyes. There are two stages in this technique that are often, for various reasons, poorly explained to beginners. The first step is to use your creative visualization and imagination. It is important to understand what this means. When we speak about imagination, we are not simply talking about the brain combining elements from our memories. Creative visualization is a human ability that allows us to create in the invisible world. Eventually these creations have the potential to affect our lives and the physical world around us. If we visualize a sphere of light, a tree, or a fantastic creature, it starts to exist in our energetic body—and eventually, it can also exist on the invisible plane as a separate creation. However, to fully succeed, you need to be properly trained. Consistency is needed to empower the result of your visualization. It will take even more to make this visualization efficient on the physical level. For example, you can create a sphere of green light to heal someone. You can visualize the sphere surrounding their whole body and increase this healing color, but you will need more energy and focus to give this sphere a long-lasting effect. So, creative visualization is about focusing on an idea, giving it a strong mental reality, and bringing it to life on the subtle plane.

In the same way, your creative imagination can allow you to "imagine seeing" the aura. At this stage of training, you can see the etheric body and some evanescent colors coming from the astral realm. The goal is now to easily reach this level of perception of the aura. After reading the first chapters of the book, you can "imagine" the aura surrounding the subject you observe, no matter if it is a plant or an individual.

We say "imagine," but strictly speaking, we are not talking about your physical vision, but a mental representation superimposed on it. You are mentally adding an imaginary layer on top of the material appearance. Obviously, now you need this mental creation to be the identical manifestation of reality. You do not want to see an illusion, but the true aura of your subject. Your imagination should be used as a key that allows the aura to be manifested.

The process is quite simple: once you see the etheric body, just imagine the presence of the astral aura. This mental representation is not a construction of your creative imagination, as it would be while practicing creative visualization; this act of "imagining" has no function other than being an anchor for realities of the astral plane. When you start to imagine the presence of the aura and its shape, you should let your intuition work. This intuition will fill out the shape you created by the awareness of its presence. In this way, colors, flows of energy, and chakras will spontaneously appear to your consciousness.

At first you might think these manifestations are pure illusions. These intuitions cannot really be differentiated from the aura you created in your mind; both seem to be on the same level of reality. However—and this is fundamental—these colors, details, mists of energy, etc. are real. They are not the result of a delusional mind. Following this process, you will have purposefully built a body, a support, used by your astral vision. It is your third eye that receives the colors and everything that happens in the aura. One could say that the goal of developing astral vision is to create a controlled "hallucination"—but these intuitions are reality, and you are aware of it.

Therefore, colors and any kind of manifestations belonging to the aura are not, strictly speaking, physically present. They cannot be compared to physical objects you see around you. They are astral manifestations that are present for your third eye and absent from the material point of view. Nevertheless, they are real.

A fundamental question remains: how do we know that this "imagination" allows us to see what is real? In a way, it is strange to ask ourselves this question now, instead of during the first exercises. But because we did not directly use the power of our creative imagination when viewing the etheric aura, our vision was no different than the one we use in our daily life.

There is a way to check the reality of the colors you start to see. When they appear in your consciousness, try to mentally replace them with other colors. If this is a genuine manifestation of the aura, the new colors you are using will not remain. The ones you saw at the very beginning of the observation will return and progressively replace the "artificial" colors you chose. This gives you a good indication of the true colors of the aura, which are always a spontaneous manifestation. This manifestation happens when you open your third eye using creative visualization.

In the beginning, you may have some difficulty controlling this whole process, but be confident in your perceptions. It is important to notice when a possible doubt manifests. When intuitive perceptions are correct, you have no doubts. If the doubt only occurs after seeing the aura, then you can consider it less problematic and ignore it. But if the doubt is immediate and remains, which is rare, then it is a good idea to continue the training on the etheric body before you come back to the exercises in this chapter.

We have now explained the method that allows you to cross the threshold between the physical and astral visions. Many practitioners find this step quite difficult. It is mainly due to the lack of understanding of the different kinds of vision. This technique has been used in a few Western initiatory Orders such as the Aurum Solis for hundreds of years, and it has been proven to be very effective. Even if this way of seeing the aura is different, it doesn't mean we cannot see it clearly and precisely. As a matter of fact, once you have experimented with this method, your physical eyes will extend their ability to see the colors of the etheric body and the astral aura, what is properly called the aura. As you progress in your training, the colors of the astral aura will be more visible, other components of the aura will become evident, and your analysis will be easier to achieve.

The two methods of vision that we mentioned before differ here. Either you continue to see and analyze the aura with your eyes open, or you do so with your eyes closed. Remember that there is no difference between these two processes—they achieve the same goal.

To see the aura with your eyes closed, you must close them from the moment you see the etheric body. (If you are working with your partner, it is important that they stay still during the observation.) Visualize the scene in front of you—that is, the physical body surrounded by the etheric. Then you should "imagine" the astral aura around the body by superimposing it.

Remember that such a process is natural. You should use your visualization and imagination as if they constitute the function of spiritual vision. There is nothing magical or fantastic here. You are observing the scene mentally, in the same way and with the same mental attitude you have when your eyes are open. You should remember the whole place, your subject included, then focus on the details. When your analysis is complete, release any mental representations while breathing and relaxing your physical body. Then open your eyes and reestablish a physical contact with your subject and the world around you.

Choosing whether to see the aura with your physical eyes or third eye should be based on which one is the most effective for you in practice. Therefore, we invite you to use both to find out which one suits you best at this level. Most of the time, the second technique is used more frequently by advanced practitioners. It is a good idea to be familiar with both methods, though, because then you can switch from one to the other when you feel it is necessary.

Here is a summary of the two methods you can use:

PHYSICAL EYES METHOD

1. Using the previous technique of stereo vision, start by observing the etheric body surrounding the physical body.

2. Deepen your observation by being attentive to details and possible colors.

3. Be aware of your third eye while keeping the vision of the etheric body.

4. "Imagine" the presence of the astral aura with your eyes open, super-imposing this "mental representation" on the previous one. Simultaneously maintain both for a while .

5. Stop focusing on the etheric body and keep your awareness only on the astral aura. Start a more complete and detailed analysis. At this point, you are seeing through your third eye, and this perception should be considered as real as the previous one.

6. Once the observation is achieved, come back to your breathing. Relax. Feel the movement of your chest as you breathe in and out. Then, refocus on the physical body of your subject. You can end the aura reading.

THIRD EYE METHOD

1. Using the previous technique of stereo vision, start by observing the etheric body surrounding the physical body.

2. Deepen your observation by being attentive to details and possible colors.

3. Close your eyes and "imagine" what you have just seen through your physical eyes. Then, visualize the astral aura surrounding your subject. The feeling will be as if you suddenly noticed the presence of the aura while opening your third eye. Maintain both the physical and astral aura simultaneously.

4. Start to deepen your observation and analysis of this astral aura. You are now fully seeing through your third eye. This perception should be considered as real as the previous one.

5. Once the observation is achieved, come back to your breathing. Relax. Feel the movement of your chest as you breathe in and out. Then, refocus on the physical body of your subject. You can end the aura reading.

Returning to Previous Exercises

It is quite beneficial to repeat the previous exercises in this book several times, using one of the techniques just explained. However, it is not necessary to repeat those related to the observation of the physical body. We recommend that you train yourself to observe the astral aura of objects, stones, crystals, and plants.

EXERCISE 12: ANALYSIS OF YOUR ASTRAL AURA

You can go forward now with the analysis of your own aura. In many respects, the preparation is very similar to the way you observed the etheric body. We recommend using a large standing floor mirror, but you could also use a wall mirror as long as it allows you to observe the upper part of your body, from the hips to the head.

INDIVIDUAL PROCESS

We recommend wearing light, comfortable clothes that are not too tight. Avoid any tension on your skin as much as possible. Wear something you like that keeps your body at the perfect temperature so you feel relaxed. It is best to choose a natural fabric such as cotton or linen, and to choose fabric that is a solid color. It should be perfectly clean when you start this exercise. If you are comfortable with it and the temperature allows it, it would be ideal to be naked. In that case, nothing would interfere with your perception.

1. Sit on a chair or a stool. You should be about seven feet (two meters) away from the mirror so that you can see your body and space around you. It is perfectly fine to only see your upper body.

2. Ideally, the light should be indirect or located to the side so that the light is not coming from in front of you or behind you. It is fine to perform this exercise during the evening using a dimmer switch on a lamp or a few unscented candles.

3. After your relaxation and breathing, start to observe the etheric body. Don't try to see specific colors at the beginning; pay attention to the density and thickness of the etheric body. If necessary, notice every significant detail belonging to this plane. Then pay attention to any colors that appear in your consciousness.

4. With your eyes open, "imagine" the astral aura, superimposing this "imaginary vision" on the previous one. Keep both simultaneously.

5. Deepen your analysis and observation of this astral aura. Observe the colors, shades, movements, centers of force in the front of your body and at the top of your head, etc.

6. Once the observation is complete, or as soon as your concentration decreases, interrupt your work and refocus on your physical body to end this exercise. Focus on your breathing for a few moments. Close your eyes and relax, keeping only the movement of your chest in mind, nothing more. Move your hands and limbs to reconnect with the physical world. Open your eyes.

7. Record what you just observed in your notebook. Your training is completed.

Repeat this exercise on different occasions and compare your observations. If you practiced this exercise with your physical eyes, it is also a very good idea to practice it using your third eye vision.

TWO-PERSON PROCESS

We recommend being comfortable with this exercise as an individual process before doing it with a partner. When you feel that you are ready to go forward, you can apply these techniques with your partner. Remember that you can use either vision technique (physical eyes or third eye) to see the astral aura; continue to experiment to see which one is the most appropriate for you.

Before beginning this exercise, we recommend choosing a quiet place where both of you can be relaxed. As you did before, make sure to choose comfortable clothes made of natural fibers like cotton or linen in a solid color. The position the observer is in depends on the duration of the practice; you can be standing or seated on a chair or meditation cushion. Choose what is the most convenient for you.

1. Start as usual with a brief relaxation, following your breath and the movement of your chest. Breathe deeply and regularly. The movements of your chest should be smooth and calm.

2. After your relaxation and breathing, start to observe the etheric body. Don't try to see specific colors at the beginning; pay attention to the density and thickness of the etheric body. If necessary, notice every significant detail belonging to this plane. Then pay attention to any colors that appear in your consciousness.

3. With your eyes open, "imagine" the astral aura, superimposing this "imaginary vision" on the previous one. Keep both simultaneously.

4. Deepen your analysis and observation of the astral aura of your partner. Observe the colors, shades, movements, and centers of force in the front of the body and the top of the head. You are now facing a real individual, not a flat reflection of yourself. You should use your mental vision to embrace all sides of your partner. In other words, you should see the aura in 3D and observe all sides of the body. Remember that the physical body is not an obstacle to your inner vision.

5. If you can, it is best to record in real time what you see. Try to take detailed notes, but do not lose your focus. Do not disturb your partner when you take your notes; remind them to keep their eyes closed.

6. Once the reading of the aura is over, or as soon as your focus diminishes, refocus on your physical body. End the practice by focusing your awareness on the breath and relaxing. Close your eyes. Observe your natural breathing and be aware of your physical body. After two or three minutes, move your fingers and your limbs, thus reconnecting with reality. Then open your eyes. Tell your partner that the practice has been completed.

7. If necessary, you can add more details to your record. Now, you can either switch your roles or share your observations.

If only one partner is reading the aura and following the training, it is perfectly fine to not switch roles. However, in this case, it is best to explain what you are doing and how before beginning. During your reading of the aura, speak as little as possible, but give indications on your partner's position and advise them to remain calm and focus only on their breathing.

ABOUT THE AURA READING

When you have reached this level of practice, there are some things you should keep in mind.

- **Aura reading can be exhausting.** Being focused for a long time while keeping the awareness of your third eye and using stereo vision is a challenge. Everyone knows that mental fatigue is real and can be as exhausting as physical fatigue. The reality is that we can easily lose our concentration without noticing it. When that happens, the brain can generate visions that are not genuine. Remember that we are working in a world full of wonders and delusions; when we are confused, it is not always easy to see the difference. One way to combat this is to keep the duration of the practice short. Five minutes should be the maximum. If you have not finished your observations, come back to your breathing, release your vision, and relax. Then go back to your analysis. You could also do two sessions instead of a long one to reduce the risks of error. You should think the same way you do when you look at someone on the street, trying to catch all the details—it doesn't take long, but it's more than the blink of an eye.

- **It is very useful to maintain your curiosity.** A strong desire to learn something new is a skill that goes a long way. Being curious means not knowing something and being eager to learn more. Curiosity is a desire that becomes energy. This is what should push you, and this is what maintains your accuracy. Reading the auras can give a false sense of extraordinary power, giving you an excess of self-confidence. This is one of the main issues you might encounter, and it can lead to mistakes and, eventually, delusion. Our brain and its ability to see the auras are wonderful powers. However, using them in a good way is like walking on the edge of a cliff. If you have too much confidence, you fall. If you believe you can fly, you could fall. Sometimes you are eager to see the aura, but you cannot. In this case, breathe, focus, and then observe with renewed curiosity. This usually helps you go forward with confidence. However, there will be situations when an observation is not possible. It doesn't matter if you are the cause or if it is your subject; the effect is the same: if you persist, your brain will offer you the vision of the aura, but not the real one. You must learn how to distinguish the real perception from the illusion. We will provide specific exercises in the coming pages that help you avoid many of the errors.

- **Learn how to record as you observe the subtle bodies.** Indeed, as your ability improves, you should discover more details in the aura. It is important to remember everything with accuracy. It may be more difficult to practice with your eyes closed right now, as you have to record your observations, but this is an important part of the training and it is better to start now, implementing this as you progress.

- **At the end of your observation, review the whole aura of your subject globally.** You started with a general view, and you must end in the same way. Clearly remember your last overall feeling. Then write down your final notes and share your observations with your partner.

- **If, at some point, your partner is replaced by people you don't know who are eager to hear about their auras, you should be careful about your presentation right away.** Do not use words that could be interpreted as judgmental or make definitive statements. You must practice empathy and always keep in mind that no situation is permanent. You must respect the freedom of a subject by carefully choosing the wording of your descriptions, along with your explanations. You are talking about someone else on a level they ignore, and it comes with a high responsibility. Remember that you are here to help, to bring light, and not to be judgmental. When you have doubt about something, it is always better not to say it. Do not make this aura reading a divination session. Above all, your goal is to bring a positive and constructive light. If you see something that seems related to a current or upcoming physical problem, do not state it as an absolute certainty. Rather, invite your subject to ask their doctor to run tests linked to your findings. All of this is extremely important for the rest of your learning and future practice. Of the practitioners of this art who did not pay attention to this advice, we observed two things: One, people who use definitive words in their explanation of the aura tend to develop their egos instead of their abilities, which leads them to an unbalanced self-confidence and, eventually, errors. And two, categoric judgments, forgetting about impermanence, tend to decrease a subject's freedom. Then the subject will accept this description as a true situation that will never change, and a problem that did not exist before can be created because of an inner conviction.

- **It is useful to make multiple observations on different people, and on the same partner but under different circumstances.** If possible, do aura readings on naked partners as well. This will allow you to see the difference between perception with clothing and without. Of course, do not make nudity an obligation, but if they are open to it, remember to keep a comfortable temperature in the room.

EXERCISE 13: MODIFICATION OF COLORS

Up to this point, you have observed the colors of the astral body without changing anything. The goal was to increase your ability and accuracy. When we talked about the vision of the astral aura, we explained that creative visualization and imagination are involved. This brain function is used to welcome the real manifestation of the astral aura. It is a way to create a receptacle to allow the real manifestation of the aura surrounding the subject. Your own observation should not interfere.

The colors of the aura are generated by the state of consciousness, the mood, and the memories of the subject. However, there is also an interaction between people if practicing with another individual. Without noticing it, every time we meet someone, the colors of the aura change. In previous exercises, we observed the exchange of energy between two people at the etheric level; you saw the flow of energy from one to the other. The astral aura does something similar. There is a connection, an exchange of energies that can affect each other.

Remember that the colors are the expression of a being. We can create, on the astral level, a specific color. Consequently, we have the power to change the color of the aura. I am talking here about our own aura; even if we can do the same for others, it is not a good idea to change the colors without knowing exactly what you are doing, as it can influence the whole body. Nevertheless, for the purpose of this exercise, you can do that without any issue, first on yourself and then on a partner.

Now it is time to learn how to change the colors on yourself and someone else. Such a modification is useful. It can help create a specific reaction on the invisible plane that can affect the etheric body and the physical body. As you can imagine, it is not recommended to do this randomly. Every action has a consequence! You must be careful every time a change is visualized in the subtle bodies.

INDIVIDUAL PROCESS

When you are working on yourself, you should start with the observation of the current state of your aura. Take the time to observe the flow of colored energy and everything that is inside your own aura. This stage of the practice is very important. As you observe these colors, your third eye is activated. You can follow the description of this process in the previous exercise.

1. Once your astral vision is established, choose a specific color. We encourage you to start with green. This is a healing color, and its use can only bring positive energies to your aura. (Obviously, if green is already the main color of your aura, you should choose a different color.)

2. Think about the color you've chosen. At this point, visualization is just a focus of the mind—you do not need to "see" the color, but focus on the idea of the color. Only keep the color in your mind.

3. When you have established this presence, start to move your awareness all around you, from the top of your head to your feet and in all directions. Then, focus on your breathing and reinforce this colored light. Increase the color when you inhale and move the energy when you exhale.

4. It is time to transition to the observer point of view and release your focus. Let this color's energy exist by itself. Don't intervene in any way. Just see this light moving around you. You are breathing this colored light. Continue this process for a few minutes, until you release any mental representation and perception.

This is the most efficient way to change a color in your aura. After a few attempts, you can try to maintain this intensity of color a little longer, and it will eventually stay on its own. In chapter 11, we will use this process of changing a color for healing, but for now, we are starting to build this knowledge. Therefore, when the colored light is felt all around you, you should come back to your breathing and release the visualization.

Practice this exercise several times a week. If you want to go forward faster, practice the change of color periodically during the day. For a few seconds, focus on the color you want intensified in your aura, then breathe and release the visualization. This is a good way to experiment without going step-by-step through the whole process. As you can see, everything is built on visualization, desire, and will.

TWO-PERSON PROCESS

After experimenting with the modification of colors on yourself, it is time to work with a partner. You need a partner to work on this skill. Only a partner can help you verify if your vision is correct. This is not always an easy skill to learn, but it is fundamental.

In this exercise, one of you, the "subject," should visualize a modification of color in their aura. Limit the choice to six colors: gold, red, green, blue, white, or purple. Then the second person, the "observer," should discover which color their partner visualized. As you can imagine, this exercise is quite challenging. Both partners are working, but not on the same thing. The subject is working on their ability to visualize and influence the subtle energy of the aura, while the observer is improving their ability to see the real colors. This is an excellent exercise to test the validity and accuracy of your astral vision. As both of you are working on different things, it is essential to switch roles after completing the exercise. It gives you each the opportunity to experiment and learn.

Keep in mind this important point: it is almost impossible to be correct every time when you try to find the color visualized by your partner. This skill is difficult at this stage of the training. Nevertheless, the goal is to help you learn. Don't be disturbed by a few errors; they are normal. Here is the detailed process you should follow.

1. Both of you should be prepared as usual. Choose the best seat possible to be relaxed and facing each other. You can practice with or without clothes. Decide who will start as the observer, and also choose a signal you can exchange later on. It could be whispering the word *ready*,

knocking on the floor, snapping your fingers, etc. Once this is done, both of you should breathe and relax.

2. The partner who will change the color of their aura, the subject, starts by doing nothing. They should just breathe and relax. The observer should follow the usual sequence to see the subject's different levels of energy and eventually see the colors of the aura.

3. When the observer is ready, they should give an indication to their partner using the signal decided on earlier. Only then should the subject become aware of their own aura. Then, the subject visualizes and spreads the specific color all around the aura. The subject then uses the signal to indicate the light is established.

4. As the observer opens their perception to this modification, the subject uses every breath to strengthen the color they chose. Keys to success are relaxation, breathing, and detachment. You should want to succeed, but don't be stressed if you don't succeed. This is a paradox, but this is exactly what you should do.

5. When the observer has found the color, they use the signal to inform the subject that the practice is complete. After a few breaths, both come back to the physical world.

At this point, the roles are switched. Follow the same procedure. At the end of the second sequence, you can share your observations. It is interesting to share any feelings you had during the exercise and, of course, compare the color found with the color visualized. Don't worry if the answer is not immediately correct. Sometimes this process takes time to establish, but you may be surprised by the results. Be patient and dedicated. Being consistent in your practices helps you succeed.

EXERCISE 14: MODIFICATION OF THE FLOW

As you have already practiced modifications of color in your aura, now you can experiment with micro modifications of the aura.

INDIVIDUAL PROCESS

Observe your aura. Then focus on a specific zone and change the color before returning to the original one. Take time to play with that. Change the location of this modification. You can also change the flow of energy, following a wave of color and strengthening it.

TWO-PERSON PROCESS

Two different experiments should be used at this point.

1. First, repeat exercise 13, with one modification. In the previous exercise, the subject changed the whole color of their aura and the observer was trying to find the color visualized. For this exercise, the subject should practice altering a flow or changing a section of the aura. The observer should find what is happening and be able to describe it.

2. Then, for a second experiment, the observer should mentally change the color of the aura of the subject. Then, the subject should find the new color that surrounds them.

After reaching the vision of the aura, always use a chosen signal to tell your partner that you are about to change the color of their aura. The observer uses creative visualization and their third eye to maintain the color around the subject. Awareness of the breath should be maintained. Inhalation is used to strengthen the visualization. Meanwhile, the subject is breathing, relaxing, and opening their mind to see their own aura surrounding them. When the color is found, the subject alerts the observer that this sequence has been achieved. Subject and observer should release any visualizations, breathe regularly, relax, and progressively come back to the awareness of their physical bodies. Each one should take the time to record what they just experienced at all levels and the color they saw, then should switch roles and repeat the exercise. After recording the second exercise's results, partners can share their findings. As already stated, it is important to experiment with both roles; you should be able to visualize a color *and* project a color on someone else.

EXERCISE 15: MODIFICATION OF COLORS IN A TWO-PERSON TEAM

Working with a partner creates a different stage of consciousness. Consider that a two-person team creates three different auras: the first two are the individual auras of each participant, and the third one is the combination of the two individuals on the subtle level. The third aura is not simply the connection between two individuals; it is the result of an exchange of energies between them.

When you observe the aura of someone, you should keep in mind that your observation is done through your own subtle energy. It is as if you are looking through colored lenses. What you see outside of you depends on your physical eyes and the lenses of your glasses. You must be aware of your own subtle body, set it aside, and only consider your partner's.

A common aura is automatically generated when two people are close together. This aura surrounds both as a horizontal ovoid. This third aura is temporary and is created after a few seconds or minutes of contact between two people. When they separate, this third aura usually vanishes rapidly. The astral energy that was created is divided and assimilated by each individual. You can now understand why you must choose the people around you with care. You share something with them, and eventually you bring a part of them with you. The Greek philosopher Epicurus explained, "Of all the means with which wisdom acquires to ensure happiness throughout the whole of life, by far the most important is friendship."[12]

This has several consequences, the first one being energetic. In some circumstances, the common aura can remain on its own for a while. The intensity of the meeting can be the cause of this phenomenon; sexual intercourse is a good example of independent existence of this aura. Instead of vanishing after a few seconds of separation, this aura can last for a few minutes. It can even be observed as an aura without a physical body. Some magic and theurgic practices use this kind of creation in rituals. We want to emphasize that such creation must be done with a lot of precautions.

In this exercise, you and a partner are going to observe and modify the third aura that both of you share. In this case, you are simultaneously the observer and the actor. Before beginning the practice, talk to your partner and choose which color you want to visualize to modify the aura, and choose a signal you can exchange later on.

---

12. Ratcliffe, *Oxford Essential Quotations*.

TWO-PERSON PROCESS

Your individual preparation should be the same as before. You can sit one in front of the other, approximately three feet (one meter) apart. You can also be closer to each other and join hands, but avoid any tension. Experiment both ways because it may lead to a difference in the third aura.

Go through the following process simultaneously. Practice with your eyes closed or half-closed. Use the signal previously chosen to move from one step to the next. Remember to switch roles after completing the exercise.

1. Start with a few breaths, progressively reaching a state of relaxation. Then activate your third eye by focusing on the center of your forehead. Do not look from the inside, but be aware of the presence of the center.

2. When you feel the activation of your stereovision and the third eye, become progressively aware of the different subtle bodies that surround you. After reaching the level of the astral aura, breathe more deeply to fix this perception in your mind.

3. Turn your awareness to your partner and observe their aura. Take the time to watch and observe while simultaneously keeping the awareness of your own aura. It could take up to five minutes to reach this point. Do not speed up or slow down the process; each of you should stay on the same pace.

4. Use the chosen signal to notify your partner that it is time to transition to the common aura surrounding both of you. To see it, you should extend your perception and embrace a larger area of the room you're practicing in. This is a mental decision that is implemented using your desire and curiosity.

5. Observe. What are the colors? What are the movements of the flow of energy? Is this energy coming from your personal auras, from outside, or from both? Everything is important. If your hands are not joined, slightly open your eyes and record your observations. If your hands are joined, you can do that later.

6. When both of you have had enough time, use the signal to come back to a lower state of consciousness, focusing again on your physical bodies. After a few minutes of relaxation, share your findings.

EXERCISE 16: THE ASTRAL AURA OF A GROUP

At this point you have learned to see the astral aura of an individual and the third level of the aura while working with your partner. You can use the same technique to observe the astral aura of a group or a crowd. This is called an *egregore*. An egregore is a common aura, the result of the union of the individuals who compose it. This spontaneous composition of a common astral aura gives interesting indications about the nature, character, intentions, and, sometimes, capacities of the group.

Using this method makes you capable of seeing the other side of a gathering or demonstration. This is the real face of a group, whether it is hiding from you or not. Whatever the nature of the group you are in—religious, political, or otherwise—you can observe what was not immediately apparent. This exercise explains how to see group auras. We have no doubt it will open new perspectives.

For example, let us consider the example of a medium-sized gathering, between ten and thirty people. You can apply the same process for a larger number of individuals. Depending on the location, discretion may be advisable.

1. Suppose you are seated. Start by keeping your back as straight as possible. Breathe regularly and relax. Listen, observing the place and the people who are there, but without focusing your attention on any detail. Be discreet. "Grab" the general sound of every voice, noise, etc. You can hear and see, but you must not focus on anything.

2. With eyes open or half-closed, "imagine" and feel that you are extending your awareness to the whole group. Consequently, your perception does not remain at the level of your physical vision; imagine that your consciousness rises two or three meters above the ground and grows to encompass the whole location.

3. Something like a cloud or fog covers the whole place you are in. People are immersed in this auric field, but strangely, it is often less noticeable

and dense at the levels of their physical bodies—it is more notice-able above the group. This is because the egregore is the result of all individuals without being specifically attached to one or the other. If you keep the observation for a while, you should see a large sphere of energy going down and changing its shape or colors. This energy is moving and can participate to move the crowd in a way individuals cannot control.

4. Let your feelings of this common aura emerge. Ask yourself: Does it feel hostile or peaceful? Do you feel tensions, discomfort, or tranquil-ity? What are the main colors? Are some colors located in a specific location? Let your curiosity drive you. Observe the movements in this aura, the flow of colors, etc.

5. When you have reached this level of perception, continue your obser-vation. How is the astral power flowing between the participants? How are they using it, consciously or unconsciously?

6. After this moment of exploration, come back to your physical senses and body.

You can later record your impressions and observations in your note-book. Remember that your senses can affect your astral vision and interpre-tation. You can fall victim to your own projection and to your a priori ideas, and this can distort your judgment. The best way to avoid these issues is to be aware of your physical body and your immediate feelings before undertaking the observation of the astral aura. An astral vision of this kind should never be entirely separated from the physical reality. On the contrary, you must be aware of the source of this aura and keep its origin in your mind.

On the other hand, your observation of this astral aura could contradict a priori feelings. If this is the case, be very careful and try to verify the validity of your observation by repeating the exercise later. However, don't be sur-prised if your psychic ability shows you more than expected. This is what you are trying to achieve and is a good way to learn more about various kinds of gatherings.

EXERCISE 17: HOW TO MODIFY THE AURA OF A GROUP

This exercise should be seen as an extension of the modification of the aura of your partner. We advise you to start with a small group, between ten and twenty individuals. The challenge is to be able to proceed without being noticed, while still being part of the group. Keep in mind that the larger the group is, the more difficult the modification will be.

INDIVIDUAL PROCESS

Previously, you observed the astral aura of a crowd, but we didn't say anything about your own connection with this egregore. Observe your own astral aura, then the aura of the group, and then the flow of energy between your own body and the collective group aura. It is important for you to devote a little time to this last observation. This is a channel of energy you can use to change or influence participants of the group. When you become aware of these waves of energy moving around you, their colors, the way they move, and what you feel, you can transition to the rest of the exercise.

1. Activate your own aura and use the channel to reach the aura of the group. The key here is to maintain your concentration for a while to see changes in your perception of the whole aura. The process, at this point, is a result of your creative visualization and focus; you should build a strong will to achieve something significant.

2. We suggest you choose a color that is opposite to the situation you already observed. You are trying to achieve a change in the reaction of the individuals in the group. Remember that a change in the emotional astral aura has repercussions on the physical level—that is what you are trying to achieve in this exercise—so it is best to use an opposite color that will allow you to observe a shift in the mood of the people present.

3. Observe this modification of color or flow in the astral aura of the group. The natural process is a repercussion of this modification on the behavior of the people who constitute the group. You might observe, for example, conversations becoming louder or calmer.

4. You can speed up this process by using creative visualization. Use your imagination to direct the energy to each individual. Visualize this light and energy going down, changing individual auras.

5. After a while, come back to your physical senses and body. Write down what you observed.

To extend the exercise, it is a good idea to change a few things, such as the number of people in the group or the location. Keep in mind that you are working alone in this practice, so the changes are linked to your own power. The more you train, the more you succeed. It is easier to work as a team, as both energies will combine to achieve the goal.

TWO-PERSON PROCESS

When you are working as a team, the process is quite the same. Together, you should start with an observation of the group and its astral aura. Then, after a few minutes, share your vision with your partner and decide on a common action. It is helpful to ask the purpose of such action. There are several ways to use this ability. Initiates have been using it to affect private groups in a positive way. It can also be used to appease a public demonstration, to increase the healing power of a group, or to create a positive impact on a gathering in a sacred place. Whatever you want to achieve, this practice is the beginning. You are exploring a different world, but you are also building a tool you can use on several occasions. Remember that your will and your visualization are the key to success.

When you agree on the specific goal—changing, for example, the color— you will take the same steps you took in the individual process, with one modification. Either:

1. Have each of you use your own channel of energy to connect with the group and implement the change in the aura. The addition of a second person makes the action more efficient. The combination of both wills is usually very effective. OR

2. Create a single channel to achieve the same goal. To do so more efficiently, it is best to be in physical contact, perhaps by joining hands. Visualize a common channel of energy. There is more in this kind of action than the simple addition of powers. You are experimenting and

learning, and consequently, your action will be more powerful and efficient.

We encourage you to proceed differently depending on the place, the time, and your feelings. At the end of the practice, remember to record everything. It will be very useful to come back to these notes and determine what was most effective. As you can see, this tool has many applications, and we encourage you to continue this practice as often as possible.

EXERCISE 18: THE ASTRAL AURA OF AN EMPTY PLACE

In the previous exercise, the goal was to feel and see the astral aura of a group, its egregore. We can use the same technique to see the aura of a place. Remember that inanimate objects and places record everything that happens in that area. This is an astral memory that creates an astral body identical to an astral aura. We recommend you start this kind of practice in a place that has a significant memory, such as a historic place where important events have occurred. This will strengthen the aura enough to make it easy to observe. You could visit medieval castles, monasteries, or chapels. You could also go to an archaeological museum; the artifacts stored usually have a strong energy you can work with. It is even easier to do this when exhibitions' organized artifacts all come from the same period and/or place.

Proceed in the same way you did in exercise 16. If you can, we recommend starting in a room without anyone around. The energy you previously observed between individuals manifests in an empty room in a different way. Either the astral aura you observe is static, as an evanescent fog above the place, or the shining flow of energy occurs between furniture, objects, artifacts, and locations. Take the time to observe and record in your notebook. Step-by-step, you should soon be ready to make a kind of astral map of the place. We recommend that you draw a simple layout of the room and add your observations. Record any details that can help you to remember the time and conditions of your visit. If you can, do not forget to come back at different times to evaluate the difference. It's likely that you become rapidly fascinated by this type of investigation.

EXERCISE 19: HOW TO CHANGE THE ASTRAL AURA OF A PLACE

In this exercise we are using a technique called *the expansion of the aura.*

INDIVIDUAL PROCESS

After being aware of the astral aura of a place, you should decide which change you want to apply. Do you want to purify the room, energize it, or something else entirely? It's your decision. Consult chapter 9 to select an appropriate color.

1. Be aware of your own aura and the invisible energy of the place.

2. Focus on your own subtle body. Change the color within you and focus on your breathing. Every time you inhale, increase the light and intensify the color. When you exhale, stop your visualization.

3. When you clearly feel the intensification of the energy within you and around you, use your breathing to expand your aura to the limit of the room. Make your own sphere of energy the center of the room. Then visualize that your energy is connecting with everything present in this room. Create links between the energy and any objects around you. Maintain this visualization for a while.

4. Release the visualization and come back to your breathing. Do not think about what you just did. It is important for you to stop and cut the link when you are done with this expansion. Focus again on your breathing and come back to your physical body.

You'll be surprised by the way people entering the room behave after completing this exercise. If asked about their feelings or sensations, it's interesting to hear what they say. This is a good way to measure the power of your visualization and to use this kind of energy.

TWO-PERSON PROCESS

There are two ways you can practice this exercise with a partner.

1. Work as a team to change the energy of a place. The purpose of this experiment could be the purification of a room or the modification of the energy present. Sit comfortably. Relax and observe the current of energy flowing into the place. Use a prearranged signal to inform your

partner that your observation is complete. Share this information and decide what action is needed. Then proceed together, as explained in the individual section. When the common action is complete, use the signal again and return to your physical body. Once again, share your feelings and observations. Pay attention to the reactions of people who enter the room. OR

2. Experiment in your home or somewhere else. We do not recommend working outdoors, as too many living creatures could affect your perception. The goal here is for one of you to change the vibration of a room when the partner is outside, waiting. Before beginning, decide how long one partner should wait outside for the other partner to create a specific color and energy in the room. When the partner enters the room, they should conduct a short meditation to observe the room's energy. As usual, partners should practice with the roles reversed, then share their observations. This method is also good training for combined action in other rooms.

EXERCISE 20: THE ASTRAL AURA OF PLANTS

All living creatures have an etheric body and astral aura. The upper level of energy that contains the astral aura can be felt or seen if you develop a certain degree of awareness and emotion. Because plants are living beings, they have a specific level of awareness and, therefore, are surrounded by an astral aura. Of course, the astral aura is different than that of animals or humans. In fact, their subtle bodies are even different from one plant or tree to the other. Overall, the astral colors of plants are generally clearer, more vivid, and calmer. The colors give an impression of greater tranquility and simplicity.

To observe the astral aura of plants, proceed in the same way you did for the etheric body. Then elevate your consciousness to observe this upper level of vibration. Try observing the plant at different times of the day and when the weather is about to change. You could also experiment with observations when music is involved. Try to observe the plant's aura, then play soft music close to the plant. Continue to observe and try to find the differences.

If you have the opportunity to be in a forest or sacred grove, go even further and try to feel the presence of invisible beings that can live close to these plants. Even if you do not see them immediately, opening your mind and perception will make you a friend to these creatures. The same is true in your garden. Plants and trees will sense that you are aware of their existence, and they will react by growing more and offering their production. This is how you can connect the vision of these spiritual bodies and communicate with this realm.

EXERCISE 21: THE ASTRAL AURA OF ANIMALS

Pets are good subjects for exploration. Most people would agree that animals are living beings with a consciousness that allows them to communicate with you and to understand your attitudes and emotions. We are not talking about a real exchange of abstract ideas, but there is a real exchange between your pet and yourself. Unsurprisingly, animal astral auras are more complex than plant astral auras. This is a good opportunity for you to progress and exercise your astral vision.

With your eyes half-closed or fully closed, observe your pet while they are sleeping. Remember that dreams affect the emotional body, which is then reflected in the aura. Observing the aura of a pet while they sleep is a very interesting experience. When you are more advanced, you can decipher a few parts of their dreams, which is fascinating. Always take notes, and compare your recordings from day to day. As was stated earlier, stay curious. Your curiosity is the key to success.

Try this work with a partner. Choose a moment to observe the aura of your pet together. Then compare notes.

Chapter Eight
BEYOND THE ASTRAL AURA

As you would expect, it is possible to see levels of energy above the astral aura. In previous chapters we described the several subtle bodies that compose our essence. Following the theosophical naming, we have explained the nature of the mental body and causal body, as well as their possible connection with the chakras. We have also mentioned other archetypes such as Sephiroth and planetary centers. The fact that you have achieved a vision of the astral aura doesn't mean you immediately see the other planes. However, following the indications we provide will help you reach this important step.

We must emphasize that the development required here exceeds a simple training—it involves exercise at another level that requires a real dedication that is not immediately evident to all. As a matter of fact, this step requires an inner psychic development and a good control of astral vision. Having reached this level of training, we cannot ignore our own inner development. It must be understood that the levels we can see are limited by our own spiritual development. The previous methods allowed us to gradually train our psychic abilities in the perception of the astral. It will draw with it a change in the vibration of our auras. Usually, this transformation occurs unnoticeably. But the astral plane involves an inner process of controlling our passions and cultivating our virtues. It is necessary to practice a real inner purification, which will eventually allow us to reach higher levels of energy.

EXERCISE 22: THE MENTAL AURA

STEP ONE: PURIFICATION

This upper exploration needs a physical preparation. We have found the Mediterranean diet to be very beneficial. This diet connects several aspects of healthy living, one of them being food. The basic principles are simple: meat is reduced and organic products are favored; caffeine, alcohol, and tobacco are reduced or avoided; sugar is very limited; and drinking fresh water regularly is essential, at least fifty ounces (one and a half liters) per day. The quantity should be increased for those who live in a hot country. Outdoor physical activity is important, such as running or walking.

Everything in your life is affecting you. If possible, avoid discussions and meetings with people you don't like. If you cannot avoid contact—for example, on the professional level—practice nonattachment. Do not watch violent films or anything that raises your adrenaline to a level you cannot manage. Instead, cultivate everything that elevates your soul: philosophical and spiritual readings, art, nature, conversations with your best friends on essential topics, etc.

Make sure you get enough sleep, but not too much. You should sleep around eight hours. Plan a time during the day to relax or meditate. This type of asceticism is a very useful, beneficial experience. We recommend practicing this way of life for at least nine days and a maximum of a moon cycle. If you use the moon, start the day following the new moon and end on the next new moon. Then you will be ready to start the next level of practice.

STEP TWO: TECHNIQUE OF THE MIRROR

This technique requires the use of a mirror, preferably a large standing floor mirror. You could also use a wall mirror that allows you to observe the upper part of your body, from the hips to the head. Morning is the best time of the day for this practice, just after taking a shower.

1. You can do this exploration naked or with very light and comfortable clothes. Avoid anything too tight and maintain a warm temperature.

2. A soft light is required. It does not have to be natural light, so long as it is not too bright. It is best to have the light coming from one side and slightly behind you.

3. Sit on a chair or stool approximately six feet (two meters) from the mirror.

4. Your goal is to ascend through the different levels of energy you have experienced in your training. Relax and use your astral vision to see the etheric body. Take the time to connect with it. Remember that you are observing your body in the mirror as something external to you. This situation can be challenging. What you are trying to achieve with the mirror is a vision of your inner reality, not the reflection of your body seated on a chair or stool. Consequently, it is very important to hold two perceptions simultaneously: first, the visions of your subtle bodies in the mirror, and second, their immediate perception within you. For the latter, you are mainly using your third eye. Keep the awareness of your inner sensations and your external vision.

5. After spending a few minutes observing the etheric body, transition to the astral aura.

6. Deepen the connection with this plane by observing the aura while maintaining regular deep breathing. Relax and breathe peacefully. Observe the colors and the flow of energy with the same state of mind you would have in front of a sunset. Do not analyze anything, just observe.

7. Once you have created this peaceful and appeasing flow in your body and mind, begin raising your awareness to the mental plane. To do this, mentally state your desire to observe your mental aura. Do this with intense focus and strong will, but without taking more time than is absolutely necessary. Then stop and breathe regularly.

8. Relax your gaze and widen it. This feeling is difficult to describe. Think of it as "zooming out," as if, without moving, you are widening your field of vision. You should feel as if you are seeing more to the sides without losing what is in front of you. Keep your vision clear.

9. After a length of time that may last between a few seconds to several minutes, what you observe in the mirror should fade to a small degree. Its reality will not feel as intense. Do not try to see anything in particular. Continue to be aware of your breathing while you observe the development of this phenomenon. Allow the mental body you are

trying to reach to manifest in your mind and consciousness in the same way that the astral aura did. It will manifest as a superimposed layer overlaying the physical body, which has moved to the background. You usually see a light haze, often monochrome at first. At the same time, you should feel a certain loss of physical perception.

10. Hold this vision and remain aware of your calm and regular breath. Then refocus on your will to see this new body more precisely. After a few seconds, release this tension. Direct your gaze into this body. This direct experience should give you a clear understanding of what we are describing. At this moment you should see shades of color, perhaps images or symbols. Observe these manifestations and remember them. It is important to record them, as they are real manifestations of a higher spiritual body. At some point you may feel a certain weariness, psychic fatigue. Continue for a few more minutes, and if this feeling persists, stop the exercise.

11. Stop the focus. Observe your breathing and feel your physical body. If your eyes are open, close them.

12. Relax for a few moments and continue to breathe regularly. Do not focus on anything. Just follow the movement of your chest. Get your limbs moving and return to the physical world. The practice is complete.

13. Record your observations in your notebook, drawing any specific shapes or symbols that appeared during the vision of the mental body.

If it is your first time seeing the mental aura, it is good to do this exercise three days in a row. After this first series, feel free to do it whenever you want.

STEP THREE: TECHNIQUE OF INNER VISION

Spiritual vision starts from the inside. Higher levels of vibrations can only be reached by an elevation of your soul and spirit. As you may have noticed in the previous technique, the transition between the astral and the mental subtle bodies is different from what you first experienced. At this point, you'll need to prepare to turn your vision inward. Revisit Step Two: Technique of the Mirror—this is a useful exercise because your brain is acclimated to it. You're following what you've already practiced, and this is reassuring for your unconscious. Consequently, do not skip the step of the mirror. It can be used as a transition to the inner experience we describe here.

You have everything required to achieve this fantastic experience of inner vision. You should practice this exercise with eyes closed, using your inner vision to ascend the astral planes. The full process is very similar to deep meditation. However, here you are very active and follow exactly what you have learned previously.

1. Sit as usual on a zafu, a simple cushion, or a chair. Keep your back straight and observe your breathing. Follow the movement of your chest and relax. Your eyes should be fully closed, your eyelids relaxed.

2. Start to activate your inner vision by focusing on your third eye for a few seconds. From this moment, your awareness should be on two things: the vision of the subtle bodies around you and their feeling within you as you ascend the planes.

3. First, start with the feeling of a light vibration on the surface of your skin. Feel these waves of energy going all around your physical body. At the same time, open your consciousness to the etheric body. Scan your physical body from the feet to the head and connect this feeling to your inner vision. Open your mind.

4. Continue to breathe and expand your sensation to the astral aura. This is something you practiced when you learned how to change the aura in a room. Let your vision expand as you breathe. Eventually you will feel that your consciousness is not limited to the physical body any-more—you *are* this astral aura. You can feel it and see it. This is exactly what you are trying to achieve.

5. Manifest your intention. To do this, take a few seconds to mentally state your desire to observe your mental aura. Do this with intense focus and strong will, but without taking more time than is absolutely necessary. Then release this focus and wait.

6. You should experience an expansion of your consciousness and dim-inution of your physical body. After a few seconds, this expansion is reversed and you can see luminous manifestations located very close to your heart. Remember that two movements occur: an expansion and a centering. It is important to notice that the centering does not remove the awareness of expansion you have. It should be as if the lim-its of your body are larger and your focus is turned inward. Once these

modifications occur, you should start to see within you the manifestation of your mental body. The best attitude to keep at this moment is one of observation. Do not try to analyze or intellectualize anything. Just observe and remember. You may feel a little tired.

7. After a few minutes of this awareness, breathe deeply and progressively return to the limits of your physical body. Then, end the exercise by concentrating on the movements of your chest for a maximum of five minutes.

8. Record your observations in your notebook, drawing any specific shapes or symbols that appeared during the vision of the mental body.

These practices are a very good way to observe your own energy without any external artifice. Even if you do not plan to observe up to the highest level of vibration, you should use this technique daily. It doesn't take too much time: center yourself for just a few seconds and feel what is surrounding you. This is a way to balance yourself and be aware of what is happening within you and around you.

EXPERIMENTING WITH A PARTNER

Remember that you can apply this technique to partner work as well. This is always a good opportunity to go further and share information you cannot find by yourself. Keep a positive state of mind, and do not present your visions and interpretations as a judgment. Just report what you see and feel. This is extremely important, as you are reaching a higher level of consciousness.

THE CAUSAL BODY

The way to rise to the level of the causal body depends on the individual. At some point in your observation of the mental levels, you may feel an inner light followed by a vision very different from what you have already experienced. This is truly the essence of the individual, and we recommend that you keep this vision and perception to yourself. This opening is often temporary and brief, but its impact is life changing and everlasting.

Later, you may have longer access to this plane, which could help you understand what obligations, moral and otherwise, ensue from the causal body. This understanding takes place from within.

Chapter Nine
COLORS AND SHAPES IN THE AURA

The aura's colors are precious indications of the true personality of the individual: their emotions, character, feelings, etc. The colors are traditionally associated with specific musical notes, chakras, and positive and negative keywords. The hues also indicate potential issues that may not be physically visible yet. This chapter provides interpretations of the colors; use them to understand and decipher your observations. Remember that you can combine this information with your own research once you have gained some expertise in this area.

When you observe the colors of the aura, you must also be aware of their appearance and movements. Colors can tell us whether someone is psychologically healthy, whether spiritual matters are important to them, or whether their life is mainly driven by human passions. The colors of the aura are very subtle, delicate, and nuanced. Consequently, we cannot comment on the countless shades. However, the important colors we describe in this chapter should give you everything you need for most aura readings because they represent the main components you might see. When you find combinations of colors in an aura, you should use the meaning of each color.

GREEN

Green is traditionally a color attributed to healing and teaching. A green aura is the mark of someone who knows how to be introspective while staying open to the world and the people. They are often philanthropists.

As some authors have rightly pointed out, when green is associated with a bright vermillion red, it is the mark of competent healers. The meaning is different if these colors are mixed, but when they are juxtaposed, both colors retain their qualities.

When the green gets closer to the periphery of the body and seems more electric, more active, it indicates the capabilities of energy work and distance healing. If this ability is used, then the green color slightly penetrates the body and maintains a more active flow in the aura.

Light Green: Light green is beneficial. This color is the mark of an individual eager to be aware of their abilities. We find this color in many good teachers. It indicates authenticity, creativity, and, by extension, the power to give birth, either to a child or an idea. The latter indicates a tendency toward the practice of philosophy. Such a color reveals a strong intuition, an inner perception of what is good and right. It is associated with a spontaneous, efficient, and humble know-how. This color marks the development of artistic ability, a use of creative imagination. This balanced vibration is a mark of taste, a love of beauty, and a knowledge of true and pure pleasures, the joys of life.

Emerald Green: This color is special. It is a feminine color that emerges from the deepest part or our being. It gives the individual a healing power that can be applied to almost all levels of the psyche. This color is the manifestation of a state of consciousness that has been reached in past lives. In the aura of occult healers, emerald green is a mark of being able to discern the real roots of diseases and existential crises. This color is also the mark of animal lovers.

Blue-Green: Green mixed with blue shows the character of an honest person.

Yellow-Green: Green mixed with yellow indicates a person who cannot always be trusted. This color is usually very easy to see and could give you a feeling of faintness.

Red-Green: Green mixed with red indicates an empathetic, well-balanced individual.

Brown-Green: We want to emphasize a very significant phenomenon that occurs when someone is lying. When this happens, you'll see a very recognizable greenish-brown light flowing in front of the individual. It is an obvious manifestation you cannot miss. You might also find individuals with this brown-green as their constant prevailing color—if this is the case, be careful.

Correspondences

Musical Note: F sharp or G flat

Chakra: Vishuddha (throat)

Positive Keywords

Ruthless justice

Perseverance

Common meaning

Righteousness

Independence

Clarity and conciseness of concepts

Logical and analytical mentality

Negative Keywords

Narrow-mindedness

Harshness when criticizing

Resentful temper

Lack of sympathy

Prejudice

Materialism

Niggling analysis

Fussiness

YELLOW

Yellow is a solar color. It is often associated with gold to represent the power of the sun. In the aura, the color yellow generally reveals the presence of the living power. If the color keeps its brightness, even in small areas of the aura, the individual will have this energy to start over. This source is always in contact with the highest spiritual powers and can be channeled for healing and spiritual growth.

Golden Yellow: An individual with this color started their spiritual journey long ago; their inner work has advanced enough to be taught to others with authority. This color indicates the manifestation of a pure and powerful energy at all levels of being.

Light Yellow: A bright yellow indicates a good listener, someone who understands and expresses empathy. This person is not living in a fantasy world—they are doing their best to be the good in the real world. This color indicates a tendency toward camaraderie, to the happiness that comes from contact with others. This color is also the mark of intense intellectual ability or activity and mental lucidity. Reason is essential, but it is not separated from the spiritual plane. Thoughts are clear and sharp.

Pale Yellow: This color indicates weakness and timidity. Communication could be hindered by a need for intimacy. Too much of this color could reveal indecision. When this color becomes reddish-yellow, it indicates a certain weakness of the reasoning, an inconsistency when answering essential questions.

Yellow-Red: Yellow with a few traces of red is associated with irritability. This color reveals an inferiority complex, though the subject may not be aware of it.

Red-Brown-Yellow: When these colors are mixed it indicates a set of unbalanced, perverse thoughts, slowing down any access to what has been learnt in the past. This is often seen in drug addicts, alcoholics, etc.

Yellow-Blue: A bluish-yellow color indicates mental problems. The seriousness is indicated by the intensity of the color.

Correspondences

Musical Note: E

Chakra: Sahasrara (crown)

Positive Keywords

Creative ideas

Enlightenment

Professional skills

Pragmatism

Adaptability

Sincerity

Negative Keywords

Excessive activity and agitation

Nervousness in speech, visible also in gestures

Lack of character

Intellectual pride

Egocentric

Bad spirit

ORANGE

When it is bright, this color shows a fundamentally good tendency. The individual thinks about others even before themselves. It indicates a certain self-control. Some believe that orange favors the emergence of the vital forces of the etheric body, giving an impression of vigor. A more intense orange color reveals a strong personality and intellectual development. An orange aura reveals a disposition toward ambition, pride, loyalty, magnanimity, firmness, generosity, and nobility.

This color also indicates a certain disposition toward communication. This person prefers contact with others through a serious relationship.

Bright Orange and Red: A bright red orange can indicate a tyrannical, ambitious temperament that is slowly wasting vitality. It is usually a sign of good physical health. However, when located above the kidneys, it may indicate a physical problem in that area.

Bright Orange and Gray: Bright orange mixed with shades of gray could show the presence of kidney stones.

Orange-Green: Orange can mix with green to indicate an unstable temperament.

Correspondences

Musical Note: D

Chakra: Anahata (heart)

Positive Keywords

Sense of friendship

Sympathy

Physical courage

Artistic creativity

Acuity of color shades

Joy and spontaneity

Intellectual ability

Negative Keywords

Ambivalence and instability

Imprecision

Lack of moral courage

Impulsiveness

Melancholy

Egocentric

Worry

Extravagance

RED

Red is the color of anger. Thus, even if this color is not dominant in the aura, it usually appears as a form of lightning, a wave of light suddenly passing through the aura. Of course, this disorder is temporary. It can also become chronic by spreading red sparkles in the aura that look like droplets. This phenomenon often modifies specific parts of the aura.

A dark red swirl over an organ may indicate a disease attacking the body. In some cases, cancer could be a concern.

Vermillion Red: This color indicates power turned toward the good. It reveals a tendency to mix altruism and action. The individual has real potential to implement change, but they may have difficulty focusing on a specific project. This color can sometimes indicate mystical or spiritual aspirations. A tendency to be egocentric is common as well. On the professional level, this color indicates an ability to manage teams. This is a manifestation of strength and passion; the location in the aura may give some indication about how readily the subject uses this energy. If the energy is located around the head, it indicates a certain tendency to impulsiveness, irritation, and even exuberance. It can lead to hyperactivity.

Darker Red: The subject has difficulty stepping back from their judgments. They feel quite capable of controlling and deciding, but their activity and dynamism aren't counterbalanced by reason. There is a denseness of energy that could have been used for good things. This tendency can lead to selfishness.

Very Dark Red, Almost Brown: This is an indication of an unbalanced sensuality. The individual may express their morbid tendencies in a pernicious way. There is a potential violence that should be restrained. They may have strong egocentric, avaricious, and selfish behaviors. This color may be present in inflammation localized around a specific joint.

Correspondences

Musical Note: Natural C

Chakra: Svadhishthana (sacral)

Positive Keywords

Determination

Natural authority

Positivity and dynamism

Strength of will

Frankness

Ability to listen, direct, and govern

Intrepidity

Negative Keywords

Ambition and arrogance

Love of power

Impatience and irritability

Authoritarianism

Fanatic belief

Tyranny

Pride

Contempt

Rigidity

PURPLE

Purple is rarely found in the auras that can be observed. It is a color revealing an advanced spiritual experience and mindfulness; life is focused on this inner journey. It is the mark of the initiates to the Great Mysteries. This color is usually associated with other nuances that help the aura reader specify the initiatory path of the adept. Purple also represents love and wisdom. An interest for theurgy can be found when purple is harmoniously associated with some shades of red.

> **Blue-Purple:** Shades of deep blue mixed with purple can indicate an interest in the occult, as well as a strong desire to keep this research private. This color is the mark of courtesy, charity, laws, and order.

Pale Purple: This color simply indicates an interest in the field of religion.

Gray-Purple: Purple mixed with gray indicates that a strong desire for spiritual or initiatory research is blocked by uncontrolled urges. A wine-purple color with gray nuances indicates a formerly sincere devotion that became superficial and misleading.

Correspondences

Musical Note: A sharp or B flat

Chakra: Manipura (solar plexus)

Positive Keywords

Altruism

Dedication

Sincerity

Love

Tenderness

Loyalty

Veneration

Negative Keywords

Nationalism

Blind devotion

Rigidity of mind

Messianic convictions

Fanaticism

Violent emotions

Addiction

Fanatical devotion to a guru

INDIGO

This color reveals a high spirituality. It is more religious than initiatory. This individual is practicing a dedicated study of inner truths in a calm, compassionate, and serene manner. Moderation and concentration are important concepts here. If physically located above the organs, this color can indicate heart and stomach problems.

Golden Indigo: Indigo indicates an attachment to religious rituals and esotericism. If indigo is mixed with gold, then the involvement of the individual in a spiritual path dates back far beyond the current life.

Rose-Indigo: The presence of a pale pink color can change the balance of indigo. If this is the case, it indicates a bad character.

Correspondences
Musical Note: A

Chakra: Manipura (solar plexus; linked to Kundalini)

Positive Keywords
Strength

Perseverance

Extreme attention to detail

Self-confidence

Discipline

Rigor

Great organizational capacity

Dignity, nobility

Negative Keywords
Too much self-indulgence

Formality

Pride

Bigotry

Narrow-mindedness

BLACK

It is possible to find black in an aura. As you might expect, it represents the dark side of a being and indicates feelings of hatred and violence, as well as a destructive desire. It is very common for true hatred to create a black aura that has flashes of dark or carmine red. Fortunately, few people have such an aura, but it is certainly disturbing when observed!

Black is the mark of something fundamentally bad that can gradually spread all over the aura. It often comes from an increase of carmine red. A real shift toward evil can occur and be seen at the auric level. It is necessary to identify this modification as soon as possible and offer options to fix it.

GRAY

Gray indicates melancholy, sadness, and despair. It confuses the mind and can lead to depression. Gray is not actually fundamentally bad; it is simply a lack of willingness. Often this color appears in the aura in the form of bands that interrupt more vibrant and active colors. The consequence is a difficulty to act and manifest positive desires. The color often indicates a sickly shyness.

When gray is located above an organ, we can deduce that there is a risk of disease. In this case, you should recommend that the subject get medically tested. A similar color is visible in the case of headaches: it appears as a fog surrounding the head.

A light mist of gray spreading in the aura could indicate the imminence of a depression that can still be stopped.

ROSE

Rose is one of the fundamental colors of the emotional body. It reveals sophistication, loneliness, fun, devotion, and friendship. In summary, it indicates a spontaneous emotional personality trait. When pale pink mixes with other colors, it can tip the other color toward its negative attributes. However, this is not a universal rule and should be verified for each case.

WHITE

White is the sum of the colors and appears when the yellow and gold are intensely mixed. It is the manifestation of a light so intense that the physical body has almost disappeared. It is the mark of individuals with a spirituality so high and rare that we meet very few in a lifetime.

GENERAL COMMENTS

We want to highlight some very important considerations related to the perception and interpretation of the colors of the aura.

The meanings of the colors provided allow a precise analysis of the aura. However, you must avoid any definitive judgment while reading the aura, as it can evolve over time. You must remember that your interpretation is true but not irrevocable. Give your interpretation but be moderate in your wording.

Remember that you observe the subtle bodies of your subject through your own aura. Consequently, your observation may be slightly distorted by your own vibrations and colors. Imagine you wear glasses that affect the nature of your perception. You must be aware of this possible distortion. One of the ways to avoid errors is to maintain a high focus.

To limit this distortion, we should also observe and analyze our own auras. Your training will help you with that. Finally, the purer your aura is, the less it interacts in your observation. Purification is an essential part of the training.

Let us not forget that we can be wrong. Moreover, our judgment and perception can be affected by the state of our psyche. We must always be careful and keep the necessary perspective before interpretation. Remember that we are talking about a body that can change as fast as your physical body.

Finally, remember that every observation and conclusion must be absolutely confidential.

ABOUT THE PERCEPTION AND INTERPRETATION OF THE MEANING OF COLORS

In the previous paragraphs, we detailed various interpretations to help you in your interpretations. However, it is important to explain the process to follow the first few times you read auras.

At first, you may have some difficulty explaining what you see, and doubts may arise. You could rely entirely on the explanations of the colors provided above. However, after several readings of these explanations, set them aside and remain fully receptive of what you observe. The key is to not limit your perception to the vision of colors—what you feel is also very important. This is a real manifestation of the energies that are directly felt by your inner self. Keep in mind that you are truly in contact with the subject of your observation. The vision of the aura is an extremely subtle form of telepathy that opens the doors to the real being. So, as soon as you see this colorful vibration, keep it in your focus for a while, and try to feel it as clearly as possible. Doing this helps you understand the nature and consequences of these colors in the personality of your subject. Be very attentive to these sensations because they contain a meaning that you must discover from within yourself. Even if at the beginning of your training you have some doubts, let yourself receive these spontaneous sensations and record them in your notebook. It will be from all these observations that you gradually build your interpretation.

Once you have recorded everything, you can compare your conclusions with the meanings we provided earlier. But remember that you should refer to the lists only after recording your own feelings. This process helps you progress in your training. If your feelings are very different from the explanations we provided, keep your record anyway and document this difference. Wait until you've performed several observations of the same subject and see if your conclusion is confirmed. If this is the case, add it into the list of interpretations.

Learn how to distinguish fundamental, temporary, and peripheral colors. Constantly check your observations and sensations before unveiling them to your subject. Always remember that the aura is linked to different planes and can be misleading.

When your ability increases with the training offered in this book, you should see higher subtle bodies. Take the time to practice the exercises with a partner before working with someone you don't know very well.

Your final goal is to go beyond the colors of the astral aura and ascend to higher planes, unveiling the true goal of your current life. Keep this goal in mind and you will avoid most of the tricky aspects of this training.

DECODING PHENOMENA IN THE ETHERIC

Auras have colored waves of energy that flow around the body. These natural movements should be harmonious and fluid. The sight of such an aura gives one a feeling of peace. However, the aura is like the sky over your head: The weather can change over time, bringing clouds on a beautiful day. If you are hiking, it is useful to know what these different clouds are and what change they can indicate. The aura is similar.

Sometimes the energy does not flow as expected. It can be interrupted, diverted, or diminished without apparent reason. Its color and density can be affected in many ways. When you are reading an aura, you can see what is happening. These observations are important, and you must decode them to help the subject. Here are some of the most important phenomena you might see and their meaning.

Densification

We have previously described the etheric and its usual size, color, and location. This vital energy can change. The size of the etheric can increase or decrease. The edge of this subtle body can grow thicker or thinner. In addition, the size of the etheric can be different between men and women. The size, velocity, and color changes according to the periods of the menstrual cycle.

We can also see unusual densification on certain parts of the body. It is sometimes possible to see a semispherical dark densification of energy. It skims the surface of the etheric approximately one and a half inches (four centimeters) from the skin. It can vary in size from day to day and is not visibly connected with the energy circulating in this body. This densification can have several origins such as muscular activity, contractures, organ weakening, etc. The process to understand its nature is simple: just focus on the heart of this cluster and you should almost immediately feel the origin. It is possible to dispel it and avoid bigger issues.

Densification can be a vortex of various colors, including red lines. In the case of red lines, it is urgent to intervene because this is something similar to a form of ulcer.

Gray flows may cross the etheric. They may be mobile or immobile. They are often caused by a loss of energy and originate from a sudden stress badly handled. We could compare gray flows to a shock wave that has shaken the energy in the etheric, splitting parts of it. Then these separated fragments continue to gravitate around the etheric like planets around the sun. This traumatic origin may be physical or emotional. The energetic charges are not bad, but they interfere with the harmonious fluidity of the etheric. Analogically, they are like disharmonious flows that can merge and create more issues. Think of these energies like solar winds that interrupt radio communications. To avoid this, it is very useful to disperse them with animal magnetism, visualization, meditation, and even light massages.

It is the same for highly energetic particles received and not fully assimilated. This can be thought of as "etheric indigestion." For example, someone living mostly in their apartment who suddenly goes for a walk on the beach or in the mountains could be shocked and overwhelmed by these energetic particles. They appear in the form of golden spheres, possibly tinged with red. It is beneficial to absorb this pure energy and to channel it to the appropriate centers through conscious breathing and visualization. If the subject does not follow this process, they may experience unexplained violent urges.

Loss

You may observe an area of the aura that looks colorless or dim. Usually, a more attentive observation reveals the energy flowing out of the body. Its density makes it difficult to distinguish anything, but if you focus, you can see a cluster made of several colors. This is a loss of energy that, for one reason or another, escapes from the etheric. It is something relatively rare.

The reasons for this phenomenon are often difficult to determine. However, just as with densification, a psychic, emotional, or even physical shock can generate this loss. Physical aggression, for example, can create an etheric injury that lets energy escape. Then, in the following weeks and months, there is an inexplicable weakening of the subject that can create a drop in blood pressure. Mood can change and depression can occur. In most cases, this problem resolves itself naturally, although it takes time. It is possible to speed the recovery using healing techniques.

Cracks

Cracks are an important manifestation of major dissociations and disturbances in the etheric. Various external or internal phenomena can cause repeated shocks, eventually breaking the harmony and balance of the etheric. This creates a real threat to our health and balance. The causes could be constant noise, violent and disharmonious music, or violent images.

This disturbance is difficult to detect. It starts with thin, dark filaments that are opposed to the most important flows; they can sometimes appear perpendicular. Then these cracks widen, eventually disrupting the natural flow. Very often the consequences can be observed directly on the psyche.

Wounds

Any physical trauma has an impact on the etheric body. We should keep in mind that these two bodies, physical and etheric, are closely related. Thus, one can find in the etheric the mark of physical problems not visible or dysfunctions that are not physically manifested yet.

In the case of etheric wounds, we often notice a kind of vortex, a cone of energy, with the center located upon the organ affected. In the case of burns or blows, the etheric colors are usually dark or dark bluish. It is very common in this case to see the vortex moving counterclockwise.

Those who use animal magnetism can work directly on this vortex, which eventually will fix the problem. We may occasionally and in relatively rare cases encounter true etheric wounds that resemble physical wounds. These could be the result of a psychic attack.

Interference

Interference is the presence of a charge or parasite in the etheric body that is independent of the subject. This is something that does not belong to the aura. Of course, there are a lot of different cases and explanations. It is almost impossible to describe the precise appearance of such interference. However, we must distinguish it from a magical possession. Magic problems are usually found in the astral aura with possible repercussions on the etheric.

Most of the time, the interference appears as an irregular, dark shape that covers part of the individual. It may resemble an octopus hooked onto the aura. You may even discover a spark of intelligence that takes advantage of one's energy. This type of phenomenon can lead to serious illness or even death. If the latter occurs, the parasite will look for another prey.

This type of phenomenon does not happen often or to everyone. First, the etheric or the astral aura must be weakened.

What we have just described can also be created by malicious individuals who tap into our energy without our knowledge and consent. However, this type of knowledge is not within the reach of most people and there is little to worry about.

We can also be parasitized by the energy of a place. The location may have kept the memory of events that took place there and infected its aura with spheres of memory that are trying to stay alive. For that they need a host, and so they use the host's energy to survive. This may cause the subject to feel an inexplicable fear.

There is, however, a positive side to everything we have discussed here; we can be influenced by benevolent memories. This is the case, for example, in spiritual locations such as ancient temples, cathedrals, etc.

Movement Disruption

We've stated several times that the etheric is a body of light that structures the physical body. Consequently, it seems reasonable that they should move simultaneously. However, the etheric does not immediately follow physical movement. We can observe a certain delay before it realigns with the physical body.

A sudden movement during an accident or a violent shock can separate sections of the etheric. Sometimes this energetic part doesn't perfectly reintegrate with the physical body. You might observe a shift on one side or the other. The subject might feel uncomfortable without knowing the cause. In extreme situations, the subject may lose some parts of the etheric, which must then be regenerated. It is worth mentioning that some shamanic practices exist precisely to find lost parts of the subtle bodies to re-create the integrity of the subject. Finally, such a shift may also affect, for one reason or another, only certain parts of the body, such as the head, arms, legs, etc. In this case, the sensations felt are related to these organs.

In some specific cases, an old trauma can greatly disturb the body without any visible disruption. The subject might only feel sensations of cold, for example. Such disruptions can be treated either by ritual or energy work, but that is outside the scope of this book.

Chapter Ten
DETECTION OF
THE SUBTLE BODIES

We have so far discussed how we can see the different levels of the aura. But there are other ways to detect an aura. We have chosen two useful techniques to focus on in this chapter: radiesthesia and animal magnetism.

RADIESTHESIA

Radiesthesia and dowsing are two very useful techniques that can be associated with the detection of the subtle bodies. Radiesthesia describes an ability to detect radiation emitted by a person, animal, object, or geographical feature. Dowsing is a technique for searching for underground water, minerals, or anything invisible by observing the motion of a pointer (traditionally a forked stick, now often paired bent wires) or changes in the direction of a pendulum, supposedly in response to unseen influences. Radiesthesia and dowsing can even be used to measure the flow coming from energy centers such as chakras. Although they have slightly different meanings, for our purposes we treat the terms as interchangeable.

We are not going to discuss the merits and validity of this very ancient practice. We assume that many of you have already used it or seen it at work. If this is not the case yet, now is the time to give it a try.

As we have explained from the beginning of this book, the human body is a combination of both material and immaterial elements. The physical body grows based on the DNA information and the structure of the energy body. Both the energy body and physical body interact with the surrounding world in your daily life. The physical body receives information through the senses. The energy body, on the other hand, perceives the various planes of the aura. These interactions are mostly unconscious. Throughout the day we react, wherever we go, to the conditions around us. Most of the time, these reactions are almost undetectable. When we walk over an underground stream, we react nervously and physically, but we don't notice it. When our bed is located over a fracture line in the ground, our physical body is affected. It is the same process when we meet someone and our auras start to react. Of course, as always, some of us are more sensitive than others, but this ability can be improved.

Dowsing is one of the techniques that allows us to amplify this often-undetectable perception in order to make it perceptible and interpretable. This amplification is achieved by using instruments, the best known of which are the pendulum and the dowsing rod in its various forms. Once again, it is not magic that makes these objects turn, but micro movements of our body amplified and decoded.

There are several applications of dowsing, but we are limiting its use here to the detection of the energy fields of the aura. We advise you to use this technique before animal magnetism, as it usually takes more time to learn to be a skilled magnetizer.

These techniques could replace vision itself. However, we think that vision allows you to observe the highest levels of energy. You could do the same using a pendulum, but we found through our countless experimentations and interviews that such a method is less reliable. When a pendulum is used in addition to the vision, it is very useful. It can be a way to verify or deepen certain analyses. It can also be a great help for those who work remotely; pendulums are the best option for working at a distance using a chart that has been prepared for such exploration.[13]

13. You can find and download such charts at www.debiasi.org.

THE PENDULUM

Before explaining the way to use a pendulum to detect and measure your aura, we should say a few words about the instrument itself. The pendulum is certainly one of the most famous tools used for hundreds of years. Pendulums can be found in all shapes, materials, and prices. This object has become so common that there are countless options for you to choose from today. To be easy to use, a pendulum must have a certain weight and be suspended by a wire or a chain that makes it easy to swing. It is good for the pendulum to be symmetrical so that its movements are smoother and easier. If you decide to buy a pendulum to start your practices, we recommend that you consider the following criteria:

Price: Some pendulums can be very expensive, so price may be something to consider. No need to spend a lot to start.

Shape: Choose what you really like. Some specific shapes are more appropriate for detection. This is the case, for example, with the Egyptian pendulum, the universal pendulum, or Belizal. It may be best at the beginning to not focus too much on symbolic forms such as the Egyptian *djed* or a sphere. As a matter of fact, they are very wonderful tools that radiate a powerful energy that could influence your perceptions. This is why you should avoid them when you start. However, as soon as you know what you are doing, you can introduce them to your practice.

Material: Take the pendulum in your hands and let your feelings emerge. Do you find it pleasant to touch? How do you feel it intuitively? Leave aside the objective criteria for now and focus only on your feeling and intuition. (This is not a criterion that needs to be considered by beginners.)

Weight: Extend your arm slightly forward without support. Does the pendulum seem too heavy to you? Too light? Try to make it swing by lightly moving your fingers. Does it move easily? Find the ideal weight for you.

Objective Criteria: Pay attention to its symmetry. This is even more important when you start.

Specialized Pendulums: Researchers have experimented with and developed several kinds of pendulums associated with sacred writings. They can be excellent tools when you are trying to go further and be more precise in your observations. You can even use them to activate the subtle bodies in a more advanced practice. You can find several options online.

Advice: If you buy your pendulum in a store, be careful with the advice of the seller. Their criteria are not necessarily yours and may not align with the way you plan to use it.

Make Your Own Pendulum

You can also decide to make a pendulum yourself. For this, it is necessary to respect the criteria stated earlier. We should note that handmade pendulums are no replacement for a very specialized traditional shape. Nevertheless, they are very good for a start.

Ring and Needle: Hanging one of your rings from a thin thread is a very good option. We have also used a simple sewing needle suspended by a similar thread. Although it is a little lighter than would be ideal, it works very well as a pendulum.

Pendant: Although we recommend avoiding symbolic objects when you're new to radiesthesia, you can occasionally use a pendant that you wear. The vibration you share makes it easy for you to use. Do not share it with someone else, as your energy is something very personal.

Crystal or Stone: If you have a stone you like, you can use it. Try to find the best spot to glue a thread or chain; symmetry and balance are very important. You'll be surprised by the efficiency of this tool. Don't worry about the material itself. The simple fact that you like it is enough to ensure efficiency.

Ping-Pong Ball: We had the opportunity to test a pendulum made with a simple Ping-Pong ball glued to a thread. Surprisingly, it worked very well. We invite you to try it.

As you can see, the options are countless, and we have no doubt that you'll find others.

MAKE YOUR OWN DOWSING RODS

To make an L-shaped dowsing rod, get a copper wire. Then cut it into two sections of eleven inches (thirty centimeters). Fold it at a ninety-degree angle, one side approximately four inches (ten centimeters) and the second eight inches (twenty centimeters). You could use the two rods simultaneously, one in each hand.

You can use the same method to make a Y-shaped rod. Find thin metallic rods that can be bent without losing their shape or elasticity. Umbrella ribs are an unusual but effective option. Tie the two ribs together with a metallic wire and you're done! Alternatively, you can of course use a simple Y-shaped stick cut from a tree, which some people choose to do.

More sophisticated options of these rods exist and are easy to find online.

POSITION

Pendulum: Hold the wire between your thumb and forefinger, with your arm slightly extended forward at a forty-five-degree angle. If you are using your pendulum above a printed representation of an individual, place your elbow on the table with the back of your hand facing up.

L-Shaped Dowsing Rods: Place the shorter section of the rod in your hands, with the longer side facing forward. The forearms are horizontal, parallel, and pointed forward. The copper wire held in the palm of your hand should be able to turn easily. You need to find a balance in which the rods remain parallel and pointing forward. They should remain at their point of balance, ready to move under the pressure of the energy you measure.

Y-Shaped Dowsing Rods: Take the two wires from the extremity that is not tied and bend the wire to create a tension. This creates a very unstable balance. This tension should be maintained until the energy measured makes the rods dip or rise.

MENTAL CODE

As we said previously, radiesthesia is the ability to detect an energy body by amplification of micro movements. When the energy body causes a pendulum or a rod to move, you need a way to interpret the meaning of the movements. You accomplish this by using a mental code.

You should pick a direction and associate it with a specific meaning in your mind. Keep questions binary for ease of use. We recommend using the following for the rotations of the pendulum: clockwise means yes and counterclockwise means no. Alternatively, you can choose a reciprocating movement from front to back for affirmative answers and left to right for negative. Rotations can also indicate the presence of an energy field; in this case, the direction of the rotation is unimportant.

Using the dowsing rods, movements will be even more visible as the two rods will rotate in your hands inward or outward. These two movements can also be associated with a positive and negative answer to your questions, but they are often used as detection.

EXERCISE 23: DETECTION OF THE DIMENSIONS OF THE AURA

What we are going to say concerns both the etheric and astral auras. This kind of detection should be practiced on others, not on oneself.

Using Dowsing Rods

We recommend using purification to facilitate the process of detection. We have often experienced the difference when practicing after a few days of preparation; your abilities will increase dramatically. When you have more experience and a good control of this process, you can reduce the preparation to a couple of days or even less. However, during your training, it could be good to dedicate a week to these exercises.

Invite your partner to sit or stand in front of you. Create enough space that you can easily move around them. Choose the lighting conditions according to the atmosphere you want to create to promote relaxation and concentration.

1. Stand about eight feet (two and a half meters) from your partner.
2. Hold the dowsing rods in the previously indicated position.

3. At this stage, the mental code will work differently from the way we previously described it. Rods are supposed to react as soon as they touch the auric sheath, which constitutes the edge of the astral aura. Rods can react either by opening or by overlapping. The type of movement itself is unimportant, as at this point you are only looking for the size of the aura.

4. Walk slowly toward your partner, forearms forward. Clear your mind. Breathe regularly. Empty your mind of all but the goal: finding the edge of the aura.

5. At some point, the rods should react. If you keep moving forward, they may resume their initial position, shift to another one, or even jiggle. Most of the time the movement indicates an opening in the auric sheath. The rods behave as if a door is briefly opened and closed.

6. You can double-check your findings by moving away and then closer again.

7. You can gain more data by using multiple axes. We suggest moving in a line perpendicular to your partner to find boundaries in four directions. You may want to extend this further by moving along the diagonals, using eight directions. You can also get a more 3D idea of the aura's boundaries by changing the height of the rods.

8. Record your results in your notebook. Try to create an "aura map" analogous to the contour lines that can be seen on topographic maps.

You can perform different tests of the size of the aura by asking your partner to use their visualization to increase the energy or change the colors. We have already covered all of the relevant exercises, and there are countless combinations. You should proceed in the same way to detect the size of the etheric body.

Using the Pendulum

The process is the same as that for the rods. The only thing that changes is your position. In the following example, we assume you are right-handed. The procedure is the same for a left-handed person *except* when using the pendulum to energize or heal energy centers. (In such practices, a rotation clockwise is energizing the center.)

1. Stand about eight feet (two and a half meters) from your partner.

2. Take your pendulum in the right hand while holding it as previously indicated. Extend your left hand forward, forearm parallel to the floor, palm facing down, fingers joined and pointing forward. This hand will serve as your antenna. Stabilize the pendulum in your right hand.

3. Just as in the last exercise, mental codes are not useful here. You can, for example, simply decide that the pendulum will turn clockwise when the tips of your left fingers touch the auric sheath. You could also decide the rotation should be counterclockwise. This is up to you.

4. Walk slowly toward the person. At a certain distance, your pendulum will react. If you keep moving forward, the rotation may speed up or change direction.

5. Double-check your findings by returning to where you began and starting again. Then do the same in a line perpendicular to the first. To be even more thorough, use the diagonals as well, as in the last exercise.

6. Alter the height of your left hand to get an indication of how the boundaries change at different elevations.

7. Record your results in your notebook.

Note: You may decide to use only one hand to detect the size and colors of the aura. This has the advantage of allowing you to record your observations in real time. In this case, you should hold the pendulum between your thumb and forefinger of your left hand and extend the other three joined fingers forward to detect the aura.

EXERCISE 24: USING A PENDULUM TO DETECT AURA COLORS

The previous exercise allowed you to detect the dimension of the aura, but not its colors or characteristics. Before moving on to this exercise, we recommend completing the previous exercises with rods or a pendulum.

Using a pendulum to detect colors is simple:

1. Stand or sit close to your partner to be in their aura.

2. Take the pendulum in your right hand. The palm of your left hand should be open, fingers slightly spread.

3. Using a mental code, focus on the different colors one after the other. Your concentration is paramount here. Each time you should mentally say the name of a color and create a mental representation of the color. If you are using our recommended code, a clockwise turn signifies the color you envision. If the pendulum turns counterclockwise or not at all, this means the color is not present.

You could also take the pendulum in your left hand and follow a chart of colors. Grids help you focus, increasing your accuracy. To find the density of the colors present, you can proceed in the same way by using a chart that goes from lightest to darkest. This gives you an accurate analysis of the aura.

If, for some reason, you must stay away from your partner, for example in front of the table where you take your notes, point the palm of your left hand in their direction. It requires more concentration, but you can achieve the same results. It is beneficial to experiment with multiple distances, as you may find yourself practicing this with someone you are not personally close with.

EXERCISE 25: USING A PENDULUM TO CHECK THE CHAKRAS

The activity of the chakras can change over time. Several books have been written about them and the need to know if they are opened or closed. This may be something you'd like to know about to complete your analysis of the subtle bodies. The following activity can give valuable indications of the overall state of your partner's chakras.

The process requires the use of a mental code, as outlined earlier in this chapter. To detect each chakra's degree of activity:

1. Stand directly in front of your partner, pendulum in hand.
2. Direct your hand toward the first chakra. Mentally start counting backward by tens, starting at one hundred, with one hundred representing a fully open center.
3. Proceed in the same way for the other chakras.
4. You can record after or during this examination.

Note that the activity detected is only measured at a specific point in time and can vary considerably over a few hours. Consequently, you are getting a snapshot of these centers. To know if the activity will stay as is for a longer amount of time, you must examine the chakras in a different manner, such as a direct astral vision.

You can use this same process to check the activity of secondary chakras, Sephiroth, or the paths that connect them. Be precise in your analysis.

USE OF ANIMAL MAGNETISM IN DETECTION

The practice of dowsing creates a greater psychic ability over time. Combined with the exercises you have already performed, your own inner energy increases. Consequently, you should gradually realize that you feel a twitch, a warm or fresh sensation, usually in the palm of your hand. This is a signal resulting from your subtle bodies reacting to the aura you are examining. The pendulum is used at the beginning to confirm this feeling, but gradually you may want to do without it, as you should.

Adapt the mental code system to your sensation. For example, by approaching your partner to detect the size of their energy field, you might choose a tingling in your hand as an indication. You'll be surprised by the accuracy of such a technique. Proceed in the same way for the other elements of the aura.

During our workshops, we have noticed that most practitioners prefer to continue the use of the pendulum. We understand that, and it's just fine; please feel free to do so. Choose what works best for you, but don't forget to experiment with new things. It is important to not be limited in your actions. Try new things occasionally, even if you often return to your favorite pendulum.

DETECTION OF UPPER LEVELS OF THE AURA

You may proceed with similar methods to explore higher levels of the aura, such as the mental and causal bodies. Be aware that because these levels of energy are very high, using external tools is more challenging.

Seeing or exploring higher planes requires us to be at the same level, a state that can only be achieved through many years of practice and purification. Meditation, breathing, and theurgy can help us achieve this goal.

Chapter Eleven
HEALING THE
SUBTLE BODIES

Once you have determined the nature of the subtle bodies you are made of, an essential question remains: What next? Indeed, seeing, analyzing, and understanding the nature of these parts of your being is only the first step. If you discover that your aura is unbalanced or creates issues for your physical body, you must do something to fix the problem. What started as curiosity and developed into psychic ability could reveal more things than expected.

Although the main purpose of this book is not healing, healing is closely related to what we are talking about. For this reason, this chapter presents fundamental healing techniques you can use if necessary. This is an opportunity for you to see how to use your new knowledge. We do not want to give these wonderful methods without the basic keys; if we have the power to do this, then we have a duty to do it for both ourselves and others. Four main ideas are important: purification, reharmonization, protection, and healing. The essential parts of the techniques in this chapter are creative visualization and mental action. There are, of course, other methods that require rituals and initiations, although they use several theurgic techniques that go beyond the scope of this book. You may discover these for yourself if you move forward in your journey.

Remember that it is important to work on yourself before trying to do anything for others. You need to properly measure the impacts of your psychic action as well as its consequences. Then, you will be aware of what you can do to help others without limiting their freedom and destiny. This is essential.

PURIFICATION

In the previous chapters, you observed and analyzed your aura. Hopefully, you understand by now that your way of life and your inner attitude have a direct influence on the subtle bodies. Several circumstances can deeply affect your inner energy: stress, PTSD, and depression can all be seen in an aura. Even if these psychological problems originated as a result of someone's life experiences or environment, they modify the aura significantly. Outside treatments such as therapy should be attempted to work through the traumatic memories that created these issues.

Nevertheless, these kinds of psychological disorders are now rooted in the astral bodies. They have created auric disturbances that must be dissolved, and the energy must be reused in a different way to definitively solve the problem. Usually, the work starts with a stage of purification.

There are several ways to proceed, and there are different levels of purification. It is recommended to use creative visualization, sacred words, sounds, breathing, and movements. But before beginning, it is important to remember what the concept of purification implies.

We've discussed the invisible bodies and experimented with their nature by developing our inner abilities. We should keep in mind that although there is continuity between the physical and the highest body, we must consider two worlds: the physical and the spiritual. To have a good and healthy life, both aspects must be balanced. This is also true of purification. It should be applied on both levels, but as you can imagine, the physical is easier. Any development of psychic abilities, such as astral vision and perception, must start with a stage of purification.

Earlier in this book, we provided some information about the Mediterranean diet. This is a good way to help find this inner balance. The important thing here is to find the best balance you can. The balance will be different for everyone and depends on your culture and your body. However, we want to emphasize that this stage of purification should be seen as a real asceticism. It requires a strong desire and will. It is progressive and requires a long-term commitment.

Your diet is not the only thing that matters. Connection with nature is also necessary to receive beneficial energies. The process is simple. All you need to do is walk outside your house and breathe, swim, garden, etc. The goal is to build a strong link with nature and find strength and peace. The pranic energy you learned how to see surrounds us, and its circulation in our etheric body is the first step in affecting the other levels of vibration.

We should now remember that the etheric body is intertwined with the physical body. The physical body is not separated from the more subtle bodies. Consequently, purification should occur on each level. Someone who has never practiced the kind of exercises we describe in this book cannot be fully aware of what is happening on the spiritual level. As already explained, something occurring in the subtle bodies can influence the physical body. While adjusting our diet, we must purify other levels of our being. To achieve this goal, we have prepared several practices you can use. They are simple but very effective. Their regular practice will give you an opportunity to clean the invisible bodies while increasing the power of your centers of energy.

Keep in mind that every time you are working on someone else, it is a good idea to start with a personal purification before moving on to the other person. Energies will flow more easily and your perceptions will be more accurate if you do this.

Many people have a tendency to ignore purification and jump directly to what is spiritual. This is a mistake. We should consider the way we live, the food we eat, and what we drink as essential. We must find the best balance in our life to liberate our mind and open our soul to the perception of the spiritual worlds.

EXERCISE 26: THE SEVEN PURIFICATIONS OF THE CENTRAL AXIS

By now, you should have practiced several techniques to see and feel various levels of the aura. Remember, there are several goals in seeing the aura. The first is to explore the invisible realm and understand more about yourself. However, I never understood why we should stop there. When I discover a new practice that can be useful, I want to actually *use* it. This is the case here.

Your new abilities should be used to improve your life. You have already worked on modifying the aura. Through this, you realized that such energy work can be achieved by activating your energy centers, the chakras.

Various websites and groups make a big mystery of this energy work. Obviously, it can become very complex if you add more elements to the practice. Some initiatory Orders use complex rituals to attract different levels of energy. Others use colors, perfumes, sounds, crystals, etc. However, it all starts with the direct perception of the aura and the ability to move its energy. Without this fundamental training, everything else is almost useless. You must build your foundation first and not the other way around, which is why this exercise is simple and very effective. It is easy to understand its principles. Energy is absorbed by our aura through each chakra and flows into the nadis. Simultaneously, a powerful movement occurs in the three main channels close to the spine. If every chakra is working properly, the energy flows easily from the top to the bottom and back up again. If something is blocked, the circulation will slow down and sometimes stop, or it is diverted. It is essential to re-create a natural flow, and your new abilities allow you to do just that.

This exercise series should be planned according to the moon cycle. The practice occurs once a day, at night, and must start the day following a new moon. The last day of the practice occurs the day of the full moon. Keep in mind that the total duration of your sequence may change but usually lasts around fourteen days.

The full program can be done either individually or with your partner. If you start working with a partner to complete the full cycle, don't stop working together or switch partners; partners should finish a complete cycle. If you are not sure about that kind of commitment, it is better to start with the individual process and add a partner once you're more comfortable.

INDIVIDUAL PROCESS

For this exercise, we recommend using the technique of inner vision. As a reminder, the full process of purification is very similar to a deep meditation, even if you are doing active work.

1. Sit on a zafu, a simple cushion, or a chair. You can also practice this exercise standing. It is very important to keep your back straight and

observe your breathing. Symbolically, it is useful to light a beeswax candle placed toward the east. This flame should be slightly higher than the top of your head. Face east. Observe the movement of your chest and relax. Your eyes should be fully closed, your eyelids relaxed. Start to activate your inner vision by focusing on your third eye for a few seconds.

2. Start with the feeling of a light vibration on the surface of your skin. Feel these waves of energy going all around your physical body. At the same time, open your consciousness to the etheric body. Open your mind. Continue to breathe and expand your sensation to the astral aura.

3. Let your vision expand as you breathe. Follow the flow of energy all around you. See and feel the variations of colors. You should progressively feel an expansion of your consciousness, followed by a reduction in the feeling of your physical body.

4. When this feeling is clear, reverse this expansion and focus on the three nadis: ida, pingala, and sushumna. Observe the flow of energy and progressively focus on the chakras. At this point, do not try to change anything. At this moment, the best attitude to keep is observation. Do not try to analyze or intellectualize anything—just observe. Continue to breathe regularly and deeply.

5. Formulate your intention of purification of the seven chakras and the three nadis of the central axis. When you have formulated your will, release your concentration and don't think about it anymore.

6. Now you should combine four things simultaneously: your breathing, your visualization, your sensation, and a specific movement. Don't worry about this apparent complexity. It is a combination occurring naturally in your daily life. Usually, we don't pay attention to it. This exercise uses this process deliberately.

7. During a few cycles of breathing, focus on the highest level possible. Then, move both arms, hands open, until the palms of your hands are facing the chakra at the top of your head, sahasrara (crown). Place the palm of your left hand in front of you and the right palm above the top of your left hand. Both hands are touching. Keep your hands in

this position. Inhale and exhale four times. Each time you breathe in, visualize a golden light increasing in the chakra. Feel the purification of the chakra as the light increases.

8. During the fifth cycle of breathing, bring your hands down to your forehead, above the next chakra, ajna (third eye). As you move your hands down, visualize and feel the golden light flowing along sushumna nadi. During four breathing cycles, proceed in the same way you did for the previous chakra.

9. Continue following the same pattern for each remaining chakra, moving your hands down: vishuddha (throat), anahata (heart), manipura (solar plexus), svadhishthana (sacral), and muladhara (root).

10. At this stage, the golden light has flowed through your seven chakras. They have been cleaned and revitalized. The energy circulating in the central nadi, sushumna, has also purified this main channel. Now the two other nadis, ida and pingala, must be purified, harmonized, and balanced. The palms of your hands should be facing your lower belly. Separate your hands so that the tips of the fingers of the left hand face the tips of the fingers of the other hand, palms still facing your body. The tips of the fingers should be approximately three inches (eight centimeters) apart. Mentally connect your hands to the golden energy in the seventh chakra and the two nadis, ida on the left and pingala on the right.

11. On the next inhale, move both hands up to the sixth chakra, svadhishthana. When moving the hands, make sure they keep their distance from each other. Visualize that the golden light is following the movement of your hands. When you have reached the following chakra, manipura, you exhale. On the next inhale, go up and continue in the same way until you reach the upper chakra, sahasrara. Inhale a last time and release both hands on each side.

12. Breathe regularly, keeping the awareness of your seven chakras and the three nadis for one or two minutes. Next, using your inner vision, extend this light in your astral aura to the upper subtle bodies. Visualize that the brightness of your aura is increasing dramatically. You can

even be more specific and use this light to clear any disturbances. You could also remove obsessions or bad emotions that disturb you.

13. After two or three minutes, release every visualization, breathe regularly, and come back to your physical body.

Do this exercise every night for one full lunar cycle. Then, you can perform this exercise when you want to or when you feel the need, no matter the time of the day.

TWO-PERSON PROCESS

By now, you are familiar with how to work with a partner. For this exercise, we recommend a standing position, facing each other. If this is not possible for the partner (for a medical reason, for example), it is best to sit on a stool. The person doing the work should be standing.

The two-person process is simple. You should perform everything you did on yourself in the individual process, except every visualization you do is on your partner. The light you are using to clean their chakras is moved by your hands. The palms of your hands should be facing your partner, between five and ten inches (thirteen to twenty-five centimeters) from their body. Your partner should be relaxed, breathing regularly, and not visualizing anything. The best way to do that is for your partner to be aware of the physical body and observe the regular movement of the chest.

When you have achieved the energization both down and up, step back slightly and open your arms, keeping your palms facing your partner. Visualize the golden light all around their aura, bringing health and balance.

EXERCISE 27: SOLAR PURIFICATION

This purification exercise uses the most powerful thing in our world: the sun. We should choose this star as a guide for our spiritual journey. It is self-evident that the sun is the source of life on the physical plane, and almost every adept has taught that the sun is also the source of spiritual life. It is symbolically linked to fire and our heart.

In the theurgic tradition of the Aurum Solis, a very simple and extremely powerful solar adoration is used and developed in practices of Mediterranean yoga. This is the one we'll share here. The best time to perform this exercise is at sunrise, outside, facing the rising sun. Obviously, this is not always possible. The next best option is to do it sometime in the morning, approximately facing the real position of the sun in the sky. Do not look at the sun directly—it brings life, but also blindness.

Individual Process

1. Stand in the direction of the sun, arms relaxed on both sides of your body. Close your eyes and feel the gentle warmth of the sun on your body. Breathe and relax. Use this pleasant sensation to extend your awareness to your etheric and your aura. Your inner vision helps you ascend from one plane to the other. When you reach the sensation of space linked to your aura, visualize a connection between the sun in front of you and the center of energy at the top of your head.

2. Inhale while you raise your arms wide open, palms upturned and held almost horizontally, though not stiffly. Open your arms as if you want to embrace the sun. Your arms should be approximately forty-five degrees above the horizon and slightly curved.

3. Exhale slowly while proclaiming, "*Ave Lux Sanctissima!*" (Hail, most holy light!)[14] Your breathing should be slow and steady; you want to achieve a flow during the whole salutation and harmonization of the sun. Take a short pause for a few seconds when your lungs are empty and again when they are full.

4. While you slowly inhale, cross your arms on your chest, the right over the left. The intersection of both arms should be at the center of your chest, the tips of your fingers level with your collarbones and the palms of your hands upon your chest. At the same time, inhale and visualize the power of the sun connecting with your heart. The light in the center of your chest is increasing.

5. Exhale slowly while proclaiming, "*Sol Vivens!*" (Living sun!)

6. While you slowly inhale, uncross your arms, keep your arms touching the sides of your body, and extend your forearms in front of you

---

14. This declamation can be in Latin or English (provided here), or in another language. It is your choice. Whatever you choose, that language must be used for all the invocations of this exercise.

horizontally, hands extended and palms facing down. Visualize your connection to the earth and feel stability and balance all around you. Visualize that the solar light is surrounding you, filling your aura.

7. Exhale slowly while proclaiming, "*Custos Mundi!*" (Guardian of the world!)

8. While you slowly inhale, repeat the movement from step 4, but your arms should be left over right.

9. Exhale slowly while proclaiming, "*In corde te Foveo!*" (In my heart I hold thee!)

10. While you slowly inhale, open your arms as you did in step 2, but keep them slightly less open and more curved, as if you offer a sheaf to the sun. At the same time, visualize that the solar power illuminates your aura, giving you joy, life, and regenerative power. You should feel gratitude toward the sun.

11. While keeping this position, exhale slowly while saying, "*Membris circumamictis gloria tua!*" (My whole body is surrounded with thy glory!)

12. Release your position, arms relaxed on each side of your body. Breathe for a few minutes, keeping your sensation of plenitude. Then, release your visualization, breathe normally, and end your exercise.

Remember that you can use this exercise to remove something negative in your aura. If you choose to do so, simply focus the solar light on it and see it vanishing.

TWO-PERSON PROCESS

You can practice this purification with a partner, but the process is quite unusual.

1. Stand together in front of the sun. Your partner will be in front of you, between you and the sun. The distance between you should be six feet (two meters), or about two arm lengths.

2. Start by breathing together to harmonize your auras and create a common aura. You learned how to do this energy work in previous exercises.

3. When this is done, both of you should perform the sequences from the individual process section. The only difference—which is fundamental—is that you visualize that you are mentally six feet in front of your body, standing at the same place as your partner. Consequently, you should perform the solar purification for them. As they are doing it at the same time, the efficacy will be reinforced!

After finishing, remember to switch so that you have the opportunity to experiment with both positions.

EXERCISE 28: WATERFALL PURIFICATION

You can use this quick visualization if the need arises. It's recommended when you are about to practice an aura reading and want to clean any parasites present in your aura. In doing so, your vision becomes more accurate. This exercise should be used only for the purpose of cleaning your aura.

INDIVIDUAL PROCESS

Visualization is the main tool used in this exercise.

1. After breathing quietly, visualize a gleaming waterfall above you that flows onto the top of your head. The main sensation you should build in your consciousness is pleasure; imagine something that comforts you as the waterfall flows all over your subtle and physical bodies.

2. This water is a divine flow of pure energy. Everything that was negative or heavy, obscure, or disharmonious in your aura must be cleaned by this loving flow. What is washed away will disappear into the earth, under your feet. During this process, your breath should remain calm and regular.

3. At some point, you should feel that you are breathing more easily than before, and the pressure on your chest has decreased. This indicates that purification has been achieved.

4. Do not keep this visualization for more than three or four minutes. Then release your visualization, breathe regularly and deeply, and reconnect with the physical world around you.

This process should not last more than five minutes. A shorter duration helps you keep your focus and allows for effective purification. The brightness of your subtle bodies greatly increases as a result of this exercise.

TWO-PERSON PROCESS

1. Stand in front of your partner. Both of you should begin with deep and regular breathing, only being aware of the place and of your body standing on the floor. Observe the movement of your chest. Your partner will continue to do the same during the whole exercise, keeping their eyes closed.

2. Use your psychic ability to observe the aura of your partner. It's best to keep your eyes half-closed. Once you reach this level of awareness, extend your arms toward their head. Your palms should be open and facing your partner approximately ten inches (twenty-five centimeters) from the surface of their physical body.

3. Visualize the waterfall starting to flow upon their head. Connect with the power and move your arms down, following the water. Support this purification.

4. Move around your partner four times doing this slow movement, from top to bottom, helping strengthen this purification. If you feel that more rotations are needed, complete them in the opposite direction.

5. Then, return to your starting point, release your arms, and visualize that the whole aura of your partner has been purified and strengthen. Keep this luminous vision in your mind for a minute or so and then release your visualization.

Remember to switch roles after finishing the exercise so you have experience as both the observer and the subject.

EXERCISE 29: THE SPHERES OF ENERGY

In exercise 26, the goal was to balance your chakras, and thus your whole body, and to ease the flow of energy circulating in your aura. In this exercise, you should focus on only one of these energy centers.

The first step here is for you to carefully evaluate the characteristics of each chakra and decide which one to focus on; you will use that chakra's specific power to give you what you need at a specific moment. You can refer back to chapter 1 to choose the chakra most appropriate for your current condition.

This kind of practice must remain rare and be used only to achieve a specific goal. It could be used for several days only if a very precise aura reading found the need. As you are still in training, we encourage you to experiment with one sphere for a short period of time. This exercise is even more important when you practice with a partner.

INDIVIDUAL PROCESS

You can practice this exercise in front of a mirror or without one. To be successful, the most important point is maintaining your focus.

You can practice either seated or standing. The point is to be comfortable and to be able to relax and breathe easily. We recommend starting seated and then choosing a comfortable position. When seated, keep your legs uncrossed and your feet flat on the floor. Your hands should be placed on your thighs. If you want to add movements to the visualization, it may be better to stand.

1. Proceed as usual with a short relaxation while observing your breath. Relax your shoulders.

2. Feel your subtle bodies all around you, their colors, and the movement of the energy. Feel the stability of the central axis and the energy flowing from the top to the bottom.

3. Focus now on the chakra you chose. Observe and feel the presence of this wheel of energy. You can move your arms and hands in the direction of this center. If you do so, keep the palms of your hands open approximately five inches (twelve and a half centimeters) from your skin. Breathe and start to feel the energy between the palms of your hands and the center. When this connection is created, move your hands back, opening your arms and visualizing this center as a sphere increasing in size. When your arms are open to the size of your hips (approximately fifteen inches, or thirty-eight centimeters, apart), release your arms to the sides of your body.

4. Keep your concentration on the sphere and, using your breath, increase the diameter of this sphere until it encompasses your

whole body. You are now at the center of this beautiful sphere. Take the time to observe from the inside, using your inner vision. Observe in front of you, at your back, on the sides, etc.

5. Intensify the brightness of this sphere. Then keep these bright colors for a few cycles of breathing. Do not exceed five minutes.

6. Start to reduce the diameter of the sphere. The light stays inside and becomes more concentrated. Open your arms and use your hands to help reduce this diameter and replace it in the chakra.

7. When you have reduced the sphere to its initial size, visualize that the concentration continues until it reaches the size of a single dot of light at the exact center of this chakra. Then breathe, relax, and release all visualizations.

In this exercise, you do not need to spread out any energy because you brought the energy back. You placed the energy as a seed that will continue to give you what you need for the next hours.

TWO-PERSON PROCESS

When you are working with a partner, proceed in exactly the same way, but moving your hands in direction to their center. They don't have to do anything except breathe and relax while you visualize and increase their power.

As you are standing in front of your partner increasing the size of the sphere, open your arms wide enough to encompass their whole body. When you feel the sphere is complete, keep your arms open and facing your partner. When the concentration of this bright light reaches its maximum, move your hands back to your partner's center and conclude in the same way. This is a very powerful exercise that combines the different tools you've learned to purify the aura.

Once you have experimented with both positions, it is always helpful to compare your feelings and record everything in your notebook. As you can see, the foundation of this practice is the vision and sensation of the subtle bodies made of pure energy, which is why the vision is important and should be followed by an active work using your new psychic abilities.

REHARMONIZATION

The exercises found in the previous section put us on the path of reharmonization. Purification allows us to reharmonize. The practices we are going to use in this section are much the same—it is only the intention that changes, and the formulation of what we wish to accomplish.

The objective of reharmonization is to put us, once purified, in relation with the divine plan and the positive and constructive energies. There are, of course, complete practices that aim to reharmonize all aspects of our being, but here the objective will be limited to the auric envelopes.

EXERCISE 30: THE SEVEN ARCHETYPES

We have explained the nature and power of universal archetypes. You know their link to the mental body. You have also experimented with how these egregores can change the nature, and even the number, of your subtle bodies. At the same time, they are a unique and powerful source that can be used to harmonize the different planes of your aura. Consequently, you must carefully choose which archetype you use to balance your subtle bodies.

This exercise uses the seven chakras to give you the opportunity to practice keeping the balance of energy flowing in your various centers of energy. We encourage you to choose a magical image you want to use for each center. You can use the archetype with the magical symbol, a color, or a flower with various petals. Once you have chosen one archetype for each chakra, you can proceed with the following process.

INDIVIDUAL PROCESS

When you are working with archetypes, it is better to keep your hands still and your arms relaxed. It is best to be in a seated position.

1. For this exercise, proceed in the same way as you did for exercise 26. Follow the same sequence, visualizing the golden color. In addition, visualize the magic image you chose at the beginning of the exercise inside each center. Obviously, this mental representation has a small dimension, as this image is created within the center of energy, but the size has nothing to do with the power of this archetype. You should see this bright representation pulsating with life.

2. For each energy center, use several breaths to increase the presence of your archetype. When you come back to the top from the bottom of your central axis, simply reactivate the visualization of each archetype.

3. When finished, relax your arms and keep the visualization of the seven centers to reinforce balance. Then, release your visualization.

TWO-PERSON PROCESS

When you are working with your partner, proceed in the same way as in the individual process, but visualize each archetype on their central axis. The images must be chosen by your partner.

EXERCISE 31: MANTRIC HARMONIZATION

Sounds, chants, and mantras generate vibrations that create very special states of consciousness. They also modify the astral and mental auras. Analogically, the sound can be seen as a stone being thrown into a lake and generating waves over its entire surface. Here, the vibration reverberates in the same way in the aura and creates effects depending on the nature of the sound used.

Mantras, or chants, can be used for many purposes, such as purification, harmonization, and meditation. They are a very powerful tool that directly activates the energy. The association of your astral vision and the use of a mantra is very powerful. You can use a mantra in various ways, but it's best to start by experimenting on the central axis.

There are several kinds of mantras you can find in books and on the internet. Some of them are complicated proclamations you should repeat a countless number of times. There are other options, such as simple words, syllables, or vowels.

Even if you already use long and complex mantras, we recommend using one of the two options provided in the descriptions of the chakras. It could be either the sacred syllables associated to the chakra by the Eastern tradition or the vowel coming from the Western tradition. Choose one of the two for the first experiment. However, we encourage you to try both and to feel the difference of energy. As a matter of fact, feeling the difference in energy depends on the tradition and the egregore invoked through this astral connection.

INDIVIDUAL PROCESS

If you can, it is best to stay standing for this exercise. When you chant or pronounce a mantra, it is best to stand and open your chest while keeping your back straight.

1. Proceed in the same way you did for the first part of exercise 26. We recommend that you continue to use the color gold and to focus on the pronunciation of the sound as the most important part of this practice.

2. When your hands are above the energy center, move your shoulders back to open your chest when you inhale. When you exhale, turn your hands so that your palms are facing in front of you. Next, pronounce the mantra while moving your hands in front of you, extending your arms while visualizing that the power of the center increases and flows in front of you and in your aura. When your arms are extended almost completely, open your arms on each side in a circular movement and bring back your hands above the center, palms in the direction of your body. Inhale again. Then when you exhale, do the same movement as if you are swimming in your aura. Proceed three times.

3. Repeat this process for each of the chakras. When finished, release your visualization.

TWO-PERSON PROCESS

When you are working with a partner, proceed in the same way but keep the palms of your hands facing their center. When you pronounce the mantra, move your hands back while you visualize the size of the sphere increasing in their aura. Bring your hands close to their chakra when you inhale. When you pronounce the sound, open your arms and visualize the light increasing.

Alternatively, you can experiment without opening your arms and keeping your hands above the center. In this case, when you pronounce the sound, just visualize the size of the sphere increasing without doing anything other than keeping your hands above the center. Then continue the exercise. If you choose to keep your hands above the chakra, do the same for every energy center.

Switch positions with your partner. You should end by recording everything in your notebook and sharing your feelings.

EXERCISE 32: SURYA NAMASKAR: A SOLAR HARMONIZATION

While yoga is not the direct subject of this book, many of the topics used in this presentation are linked to this tradition. For those who are unfamiliar, yoga is the practice of asanas (poses) using the body and conscious breathing. Yoga has many aspects. It is a mind-body-spirit practice, not only a physical practice. The movements strengthen your physical body, but yoga also promotes meditation, body stretching, breathwork, songs and mantras, and much more. These facets of yoga help you to develop your consciousness and your well-being, eventually finding harmony and balance in your whole being and in your life.

There are several levels in yoga. Tantra yoga is an esoteric practice, and its teachings go beyond mainstream yoga. Reiki, which is quite popular today, focuses on a kind of energy work. However, this is a very late transplant that can be interesting for those who have not explored tantric practices yet.

A lesser-known type of yoga stems from the Mediterranean tradition. The origin is fascinating and was described by Plutarch. To summarize, we don't know about individual travels, but we know for certain that Alexander the Great met with yogis when he came to the Indus Valley. These yogis were called "gymnosophists" by Plutarch.[15] Several conversations have been reported, and they are all interesting. When Alexander travelled back to Alexandria, he invited a few yogis to join him. We now know about their presence in Egypt and Greece. We also know that such practices and parts of the philosophy were introduced in philosophical circles and were eventually incorporated to some secret societies in antiquity.

As you have discovered, the practice of visualization opens a vast array of possibilities. Associated to asanas and energy work, it allows you to increase your energy as a whole. We invite you to use the benevolent power of the color golden yellow and the power of the sun in a very famous asana called Surya Namaskar, the sun salutation.

---

15. Plutarch, *The Parallel Lives*, 64–65.

INDIVIDUAL PROCESS

The stages of this asana are described in this section. If you are a visual learner, you can also easily find videos of this asana on the internet. Our description corresponds to Surya Namaskar A (there are three main versions of the sun salutation, with several variations). This is the one we recommend.

1. Stand in mountain pose (Tadasana). In this pose your feet are parallel, aligned with the knees and hips. Your hands are together on your heart, palms together and tips of the fingers directed toward the sky. This is called Anjali mudra. *(Visualization: Take time to breathe and visualize a horizon in front of you. Choose scenery you like and where you feel comfortable. The sun is about to rise, and its light is almost visible.)*

2. On an inhale, extend your arms toward the ceiling, keeping the palms together. Roll your head back. *(Visualization: The light of the rising sun increases, even if you do not see the sun yet.)*

3. On an exhale, fold forward. Bend your knees as needed. Relax your head. This position is called Uttanasana. *(Visualization: The sun starts to appear above the horizon. A powerful energy flows toward you and upon the back of your head.)*

4. Inhale halfway, hands resting on your shins or on the floor. Close your eyes. *(Visualization: The heat of the sun moves on the top of your head. As you inhale, the energy flows in your central nadi, sushumna.)*

5. Exhale and move your left foot backward, followed by your right foot, into high plank pose. Align your shoulders above your wrists. Heels press back so you are resting on the balls of your feet. *(Visualization: As you align your spine, the energy flows to the chakra at the bottom of your spine. At the same time, your aura is filled with golden light from your head to your feet.)*

6. Shift your shoulders forward slightly for the next position, Chaturanga. *(Visualization: The sun is now fully above the horizon, and you touch the ground with respect.)*

7. On an exhale, lower halfway down, keeping your elbows close to your ribcage. Your shoulders should be the same level as your elbows. Keep

your shoulder blades back and down, your elbows at a ninety-degree angle, your forearms perpendicular to the floor, and your upper arms parallel to the floor. *(Visualization: The previous visualization is strengthened.)*

8. Engage all your muscles and keep your upper body and legs above the floor. Pause for a moment, keeping everything engaged. *(Visualization: Your whole body is surrounded by the golden light.)*

9. On an inhale, press into your hands and the tops of your feet. Extend your legs, straighten your arms, and open your chest for upward-facing dog. This position is called Urdhva mukha svanasana. *(Visualization: The power at the bottom of your spine, in the lowest chakra, starts to rise along the ida and pingala nadis.)*

10. Pause for a moment, keeping everything engaged. *(Visualization: While you breathe, the flow of energy reaches the top of your head. Maintain the visualization of the sun and continue to welcome its energy with respect.)*

11. Firmly press your hands into the floor and lift your hips upward, lengthening your spine for downward-facing dog. Push your heels down. With your head hanging heavy, look at your feet. *(Visualization: You are now a bridge of golden light, firmly rooted to the earth.)*

12. Continue to push into your hands and take a few breaths. *(Visualization: Maintain the vision of the sun, now higher in the sky.)*

13. Lift the left leg up, then step forward, with your hands now framing your left foot. Step forward with your right foot, feet now parallel. Alternatively, you could bend your legs and jump to your hands; such movement should be light and ethereal. *(Visualization: You are getting closer to the sun. Feel the warmth of the star on your whole body.)*

14. On an inhale, place your hands on your shins or on the floor. *(Visualization: The top of your head is warmer now.)*

15. Fold forward, keeping your knees bent as needed, neck relaxed and head down. *(Visualization: Keep the vision of the golden light surrounding you and the sun rising in front of you.)*

16. On an inhale, using your core, reach up and extend your arms above your head. Look to your thumbs. *(Visualization: Strengthen the visualization of your three nadis, which are empowered and vibrating. Above your head a golden sphere shines around the chakra.)*

17. Exhale and return your hands to your chest in Anjali mudra, as you did to start the asana. *(Visualization: You are now surrounded and immersed in the golden light that filled your whole aura. The sun is in front of you, and you see its rays connected with your aura. After a few breaths, release your visualization.)*

18. If you can, repeat the asana three times. Follow the same sequence and visualization, except for the fifth step. The second time you perform the asana, you should move your right foot backward first. The third time, you should jump, with both legs flying to the back to reach the plank position.

TWO-PERSON PROCESS

In this practice, your partner should sit on a cushion after having practiced a relaxation. Throughout this process, they should remain in silence and in a state of mindfulness.

Set up your yoga mat so you are facing your partner. Before beginning your three sun salutations, you must mentally dedicate your practice to your partner. In simple words, mentally state that you want to bring your partner the power of the sun, health, harmony, and energy. Then proceed to your practice, visualizing the sun above their head and the modifications of their aura.

At the end of the asana, sit in the same way as your partner. Then, both of you should end with a short practice of Pranayama.

PROTECTION

For a very long time I thought psychic protection was unnecessary. My thinking was that someone who is doing his best to have a healthy physical and spiritual life was protected automatically. However, an elevated level of vibration places you at risk. When you follow a psychic or spiritual training, your aura and centers of energy radiate at a higher frequency. Imagine a slowly turning spoked wheel. If you throw a stone through it, the stone has a good chance of passing through. But if the wheel is turning faster, the chance is higher that the stone will be rejected. I believed that my inner center worked the same way, like a wheel spinning faster to reject more threats, and that I was protected. The vision of my astral aura corroborated that. However, I was forgetting an important thing: malicious people can be strong too! In the same way that an excellent martial artist may attract the attention of a stronger one, our aura can attract harmful influences without our knowledge. Traumas from our past experiences and locations can let in threats that disturb the correct circulation of energy. You have already started to clean parts of this type of active memory, but it is essential to limit their presence further, keeping only the best resolutions.

Some time ago I was called by a woman who had difficulty sleeping, recurrent difficulty breathing, and many psychic manifestations in her house. Medical exams didn't reveal anything that could indicate an origin for these phenomena. As a matter of fact, the psychic manifestations were coming from a different source. I met her in her living room and, after a few minutes of discussion, began an aura reading. She was a very strong-willed Italian woman, and I was surprised by the results. I saw a very powerful aura she had built as a circle of protection, which was keeping both positive and negative influences out—an almost impenetrable oval. Over the years, she had developed a very effective creative visualization, and this was the cause of the barrier. Consequently, she was suffocating on the invisible level because positive energies were being rejected along with negative. This is something that can be changed with specific astral work, but first the practitioner must be aware of the situation. I used techniques of magnetism and visualization to open this invisible barrier, and in a few minutes she was breathing again and started her recovery.

So, it is essential to elevate our soul and increase our energy, but it is prudent to practice some methods of protection as well. This is just common sense.

EXERCISE 33: THE LOTUS FLOWER

The lotus is a powerful symbol used in several ancient cultures. This beautiful flower is associated with the idea of creation. It is the symbol of the soul rising above the body to reach illumination. In the yoga tradition, a lotus is used to symbolize the chakras, the number of petals being different for each one. For a very long time, tantric traditions and theurgic practices have used this archetype for protection. A combination of creative visualization, breathing, and inner vision are the keys that must be used to succeed. Because you have changed the nature of the aura in previous exercises, you have trained yourself for these advanced practices. The goal of this exercise is to use the very powerful symbol of the flower as an inner protected space.

The process is quite simple. After visualizing the lotus, you will move your consciousness within the flower you choose. This is not an out-of-body experience—on the contrary, this is an inner-body experience. After training with this exercise several times at your own pace, you should be able to achieve this in a few seconds. You must remember that the purpose of this exercise is protection. It is possible to obtain an effect that lasts a long time by repeating the same exercise several times, but you can also use it as the situation requires. Everything is based on your inner vision and your concentration, allowing your consciousness to move to a specific point in your subtle body without losing the perception of your physical body as a whole.

For this exercise, we recommend using a chakra we briefly mentioned in chapter 1. Anahata is usually described as the heart's chakra, but as a matter of fact, there is a secondary chakra linked to the heart that is situated slightly below the heart. Its name is *hrit chakra*. It is one of the most powerful chakras for protection purposes. Hrit chakra is sometimes known as the *surya* (sun) *chakra*. Its role is to absorb energy from the sun and provide heat to the body and the other chakras (to manipura, in particular), to which it provides *agni* (fire).

Hrit chakra has three regions: a vermillion sun region, within which is a white moon region, within which is a deep-red fire region. Within this is the red wish-fulfilling tree, *kalpavriksha*, which symbolizes the ability to manifest what one wishes to happen in the world. The chakra is the only one related to the number eight, a powerful spiritual number that can be found at the heart of the most occult spiritual traditions.

After using hrit chakra several times, you can explore other possibilities by moving your consciousness to another energy center. Do not do more than one at a time. Notice the differences while keeping the specific character of each chakra in mind.

INDIVIDUAL PROCESS

As in most of the exercises provided in this book, you should start this one with a short relaxation, awareness of your breathing, and the inner vision of your subtle bodies.

1. After reaching the astral aura, keep this vision in your mind and feel the waves of energy flowing around you. After a couple of minutes, focus on your central axis and the seven chakras. They should be rotating, the energy flowing in and out and the nadis pulsating life.

2. Breathe more deeply and move your consciousness to the central chakra, anahata. Do not try to visualize anything related to this center; just focus on your memory of this center. When you feel the energy in this chakra as a warmth in your chest, use the channel between anahata chakra and hrit chakra. Think about the number of petals, the colors, and the location in your chest. Remember the power of the sun associated to it.

3. At this stage of the exercise, you should be using your inner vision, focus, and breathing to move your consciousness from your brain to the center you are focusing on. When you feel a modification of consciousness, losing your previous awareness and feeling that you have moved into the heart chakra, visualize that you are sitting in the center of the lotus. The eight petals are around you. The flower is neither fully open nor fully closed. You are seated inside this flower. Take time to look around and count the petals. Look at the sky above your head and feel that you are separated from the earth. When everything has been built around you by your creative visualization, remember all of the details and continue to breathe, keeping a vivid sensation of this scenery.

4. Visualize that the petals of the lotus are shining. Their light is increasing and they are moving slightly. Continue to breathe and visualize that this flower is increasing in size until it is surrounding your whole body, with you standing in the center. This flower is your protection.

5. Inhale and move your consciousness back to your forehead. Keep this intense visualization for a few minutes.

6. Decrease the size of the lotus to return to the initial perception within your heart. Focus again on your breathing and the movement of your chest. Then, progressively come back to your physical body. Once again, observe the waves of energy moving around you and open your eyes.

TWO-PERSON PROCESS

When you are working with a partner, ask them to be aware of their physical body and observe their breathing while relaxing.

You should follow the same process you just experimented on yourself. However, this time visualize the full exercise on your partner. It is good to use and move your hands toward the energy center to help you focus. At the same time, this movement will help you move the energy and activate the center itself. Do not exceed five minutes when performing this exercise.

EXERCISE 34: THE WALL OF LIGHT

Walls have been used for centuries to protect against adversaries or threats of various kinds, visible or invisible. It is obvious that our subtle bodies can feel more than the physical level; for example, it's possible to feel uncomfortable even if nothing on the physical level is noticeable. Humans have a kind of instinct that warns us from something immaterial. This is why, for a very long time, magical circles have been used for protection and invocation.

At this stage, there is no need to learn a complex magical ritual to start using this principle. Your own aura can become a real wall of light protecting you—but you must be careful. As mentioned earlier, a strong visualization can create an impenetrable barrier that would separate us from the world. This situation could become very negative, repelling good vibrations. Consequently, it is better to use a wall to filter the nature of energy we want to receive. We are not trying to fight evil spirits, but to select which powers will be inside the space we are creating. Such walls work like a screen on a window.

You must not make your wall totally impervious to the outer world. We need a clean energy to give us an inner power that can help us grow. Even if this kind of filter works, the best protection is our own integrity and morality. On the magical and spiritual levels, being a good person is the best protection we can build.

In this exercise, you are using a specific part of your aura to build a wall of light, becoming the filter you need. After learning this simple process, use it when you feel something threatening, either spiritual or material. Nevertheless, even as a filter, we do not recommend keeping this wall of light up all the time. Use it only when you need it.

INDIVIDUAL PROCESS

No special preparation is needed for this exercise. You can practice either seated or standing. It is good to face east the first few times you perform the entire process. Eventually, you will be able to do this exercise wherever you are.

1. After a short relaxation, use your inner vision to progress step-by-step from your physical body to your astral aura.

2. As you may remember, beyond the astral aura's periphery is a very thin auric sheath or auric envelope. You'll be using this zone of the aura to increase its natural functions of filtering and protecting.

3. Keep your awareness of the flow of colored energy moving in your aura. It is useful to contemplate this light from within as you breathe regularly. Doing so helps you extend your sensation to a larger size until you feel the presence of the empty space without color. Nothing seems to flow in this zone. You should feel only silence and emptiness.

4. The next action you need to take to build protection could be seen as paradoxical: you need to enjoy your focus on this space. This emotion works like a tool, strengthening this zone of your aura. Everything sent from outside should cross this area of the aura. Do not exceed four or five minutes exploring this zone all over your body.

5. A denser membrane will be next to the astral aura and on the exterior. It is usually a beige color. In this exercise, you should add a golden color with the intention of filtering everything coming from outside. We've found it useful to focus on a small area of the sheath in front of the forehead. Once you have created this color and focused on the idea of the filter, progressively extend this golden zone to the entire surface of your sheath. It will become a real shield. Then, keep the whole surface in your mind while you breathe and formulate a clear intention to keep this filter for the next eight hours. You should feel a real tension

in your mind, a consequence of your concentration. Keep this feeling for two or three minutes, then release it.

6. Progressively come back to the sensation of your physical body and eventually release all visualization.

As part of your training, the first time you practice this exercise, we recommend practicing daily for one week. This is the best way to build this filter and remember the sensations associated with it. After one week of practice, it will be easier for you to reactivate this filter rapidly when needed.

TWO-PERSON PROCESS

We recommend working with your partner only after seven weeks of individual practice. The two-person process is a very good opportunity to test this filter using several options.

If there are no physical issues, choose a standing position. You and your partner should stand face-to-face, approximately six feet (two meters) apart. Here are different scenarios you can use to experiment together.

Position the Density of the Shield: After your partner has strengthened their shield, extend your arms in front of you. Move slowly in your partner's direction, right hand open, until you feel the surface of the aura of your partner. When you feel it, continue to use your right hand to explore the whole surface. Try to feel if some parts are thinner or thicker. During this examination, your partner should keep their eyes closed.

Resistance of the Shield: Proceed in the same way as before, but when you are in contact with the shield of your partner, imagine you push it with your hand to test its resistance. Do that in several places. When this is done, exchange your feedback.

Perception of an Attack: Your partner builds their shield and maintains its density. Place your hands in front of you, palms facing each other, about eight inches (twenty centimeters) apart. Visualize a sphere of dark red light. Increase the density of the color while breathing. When the sensation of the sphere is clear, move both hands in a single movement in the direction of your partner. At the same time, visualize the sphere going through their shield. Observe the reactions of your partner. If the sphere goes through, wait a few seconds, then extend your arms, palms facing your partner, and recall the sphere. Disperse the energy by shaking your hands, as if you are removing any particles of this energy.

Emptiness as Protection: Ask your partner not to focus on the sheath and shield, but to focus on the empty space surrounding their astral aura. Ask them to imagine that this emptiness is working as a protection against any external negative energy. As for the first option, use your hands to observe and test this shield.

Remember to switch roles to experiment with both positions.

HEALING

Once the detection and analysis of the aura is done, you can focus on changing things that limit your abilities. This requires control of the astral energy, and therefore the practice of animal magnetism. In this section, we will give you some elements to help you understand how it works, and then you can continue with individual experiences.

In previous chapters we explained how to see the etheric from your hands and how to detect the aura through radiesthesia. You discovered that it was not only possible to see the aura, but also to "touch" it and to feel it. To go further, it is necessary to be able to detect the aura whenever you want.

As previously discussed, your hand radiates etheric and astral energy. The latter can be directed to a precise target. So, if you point your fingertips at someone's forehead, they will feel the energy very distinctly. But often the sensation is first perceived at the level of the aura, of the etheric, like a breath or a draft of wind. You can also do these experiments and trainings by asking your subject to close their eyes. It is good to try experimenting at different distances and on different parts of the body.

From there, it follows that your action can have a real influence on individuals. You can use the energy that comes out of your fingers or out of your hand. If you observe a conical depression, this may mean that the etheric aura has been affected. Seeing such a manifestation in the aura usually indicates a sickness that could be treated by mesmerism. You can use movements called *passes* to dissolve this astral manifestation. Doing so will have a repercussion on the physical body. The same is true for cracks in the aura, passed memories, engrams, etc. It is possible to "reweave" the aura with your fingertips, just as you would do for embroidery. You can practice some of these actions on yourself, but not all; some of them are too complex to perform directly. We encourage you to try various techniques and find out what it is possible for you to do.

EXERCISE 35: MESMERISM

Healing with human energy has been used forever and is still used today, with various fancy, exotic words. The basis of these techniques is the same: energy.

Between the eighteenth and twenty-first centuries, this was referred to as *magnetism*. We know today that our physical body is not magnetic in the same way as a magnetic piece of metal—we cannot attract metal or anything of the sort. However, another kind of energy surrounds us and, as we just explained, we can use it.

We now invite you to increase your healing energy using visualization in a spiritual journey. Then, use that energy when you need it.

INDIVIDUAL PROCESS

I recommend you include deep relaxation in your journey. It is good to perform this exercise once a week, or when you feel you need more energy. When you are practicing alone, you can either:

- Record yourself reading the journey aloud and listen to it during relaxation,
- Perform relaxation in a seated position with your eyes slightly open, reading the journey aloud in a slow, deep voice, OR
- Listen to recordings. They are offered at www.debiasi.org from time to time.

JOURNEY

After being in the state of relaxation, you can continue with the following:

You stand outside, in a natural space. You can turn your head in one direction and then the other. Take the time to look around, to look at the ground. Let your gaze travel in all directions. Feel the stability of the earth under your feet. Now look ahead.

A sphere of light, very close to the surface of the earth, is appearing. This golden light does not yet allow us to see what it contains. You only observe this pulsating, luminous sphere. Continue to focus on this light and breathe.

Gradually, you become more and more aware of the feeling of the ground under your feet. On your left is a garden of fragrant herbs. You can see the plants gently shaking in a light breeze. You can smell rosemary, thyme, and many other aromatic herbs. This fragrant herb garden is surrounded by old olive trees with gnarled trunks. Their foliage shakes slightly with the gentle movement of the air.

In front of you, gentle green hills stretch out to the horizon. The sky is blue, dotted with a few clouds so light that they seem like feathers stretched out on this celestial vault. Turning your head to your right, you see a row of cypress trees stretching out toward the horizon, following the contours of the land. Take the time to look around you, to look at the ground, the scenery, the sky. Gaze in all directions. Feel the stability of the earth beneath your feet. Lift your eyes to the horizon in front of you.

Gradually, particles of light resembling fireflies begin to come out of the ground and swirl in a harmonious dance. They look like bees hovering over flowers. They gradually rise to a height that is approximately double your own height. Their dance widens and their density increases significantly. This vision fascinates you. These particles of living light are now forming a sphere of light whose outlines are beginning to take shape. Its density increases while retaining its transparency. This luminous sphere is brilliant and animated with a pulse of life.

Keep focusing on that light and breathing. This sphere increases in diameter and is approaching. You are fascinated by its luminosity, which now fills the entire field of your vision. It positions itself in front of you. You feel even more clearly its soothing vibration, its pulsation of life, and sweetness.

You have now decided to go ahead and continue your journey.

Taking a step forward, you enter the sphere.

Once inside, it feels huge, and you breathe more deeply. Your consciousness expands and a different landscape begins to emerge in front of you. A mysterious door opens, revealing a path of fine golden sand shimmering under a soft and peaceful sun. On the right of this trail and like a superimposed vision, you continue to see the row of cypress trees, the tips of which gently wave in the breeze. The delicate sandy path in front of you seems to lead to a distant little edifice reminiscent of a square temple.

You approach this building, which is truly an antique and harmonious square, marble temple. A gallery around it is supported by a colonnade on all four sides.

In the middle of the wall, a dark wooden door is currently closed.

Get closer to this door. Take the time to breathe and feel the calm of this place, its stability and harmony.

Then, after a few breaths, knock several times on the door to request entry.

A silence follows, but you feel that something is going to happen.

Slowly, silently, and with a steady movement, the door opens.

The difference in light prevents you from immediately seeing what is inside. Cross the threshold of the temple.

Gradually, your vision becomes accustomed to the interior of the place. You are in a single room with natural stone walls made of large blocks of marble. The ground is made of large slabs of stone smoothed by the passage of all those who have visited this place.

In the center, there is a simple cube of polished stone. Walk toward it.

Its upper surface is approximately at the height of your knees.

I invite you to sit on this stone cube, facing the entrance door.

You feel the soft freshness of the stone when you sit down. Your feet are on the floor, your legs parallel, and your hands flat on your thighs.

Breathe and relax.

There is an opening in the center of the roof, and a ray of light descends vertically on this cube. Fine particles of light dance in this cylinder of light.

Everything is peaceful. You feel calm and serene. This space is clearly outside the realm of time.

The connection with this throne of stone is increasing. The serenity and stillness of this place begins to change your level of vibration.

Your breathing is still slow, deep, and harmonious. You feel the gentle warmth of the cone of light descending upon you, warming the top of your head.

Your feet are rooted to the ground. Energy from the sun enters the top of your head and travels down your energy channels, illuminating each of your energy centers, your chakras. Your body of light is gradually transfigured, illuminated as you continue to breathe peacefully. All around you reign peace, stability, and harmony. This stability gives you strength, power, and health.

With each breath, this feeling of power and peace increases. This beneficent golden light invigorates all parts of your subtle being associated with the stability manifested by the stone cube on which you are sitting.

You are rooted in the foundation of this temple, in the earth itself. The flow of energy brought by the rays of the sun goes through you. You can feel this channel through your feet to the center of the earth. You are gradually communicating more clearly with the consciousness and wisdom of the earth.

I will now pronounce the earth mantra "LAM" five times. This mantra will help you to deepen your connection with this element and to seal within you this peace and stability.

Now feel the energy rising from the earth to your subtle body, your light body. It passes through your feet and the stone cube, and it is concentrated at the bottom of your spine, where the tantric force of your Kundalini is located.

You feel more clearly this concentration of energy, which is at the same time powerful, peaceful, and beneficent. Your breathing is still regular and harmonious.

Shift your awareness to the top of your head. The sunlight enters, carried by your breath, and descends to the center of your chest. There arises and grows an intense desire for life and peace, for health and harmony, a desire for fulfillment and transfiguration.

The rise of this desire makes the sensation at the bottom of your spine sharper. As you breathe in, see and feel now this energy of the Kundalini starting its vertical ascent, rising toward the heart chakra.

Feel this circulation in all the energy channels inside your psychic body.

Feel your organs, your bones, their solidity; the beauty, the strength of your skin; stability, solidity.

Feel the ideal, the archetype, of an illuminated, transfigured, transformed physical body, in perfect physical and energetic condition.

Breathe that solidity.

End the relaxation in your usual way.

TWO-PERSON PROCESS

When you work with your partner, the process is to guide them in the relaxation and the journey. Then, at another time, switch roles.

Chapter Twelve

SEEING THE AURA AT A DISTANCE

Using the expression *action at a distance* refers to two different things that allow two different types of action. First, it could refer to energy work based on the limits of the subtle bodies, using a traditional process called *radionics* or *electromagnetic therapy*; this is the action we will experiment with in this chapter. The second action is based on characteristics of subtle bodies that can, under special circumstances, separate from the physical body and travel in the astral realm, which we will describe in chapter 13.

The aura has a frequency that gives it a unique character. Previously, we used the metaphor of concentric undulations on the surface of a lake. Strictly speaking, the size of our aura has no limit. Consequently, our aura is present, in one way or the another, throughout the entire Universe. Every place on the surface of the planet contains auras of every human being. All of these energetic fields are intertwined, but not merged. In the same way, radio waves and television signals are always present and are only revealed when you use a receptor to tune in. If we keep the same analogy, we understand that a receptor is needed to use these waves, as well as a way to select the correct channel. This is what radionics refers to as a witness.

A witness is a physical element belonging to an individual. It could be a strand of hair, a nail, a few drops of saliva, etc. This witness is placed or taped on a square of white paper. On the other side of the paper, the individual has written their full name and date of birth in black ink. This is what constitutes the witness, which creates a living link with the person's auras, no matter the distance.

Now, it is necessary to use a receptor to select the specific aura of the individual you want to observe or treat at a distance. Traditionally, a decagon drawn on a white page is used for this purpose. This drawing is placed on a table with the witness in the center of it. When such preparation is done, only the aura of the individual remains inside this geometric figure, all of the other auras being removed. When everything is in place in such a way, it is possible to do an aura reading, or almost any kind of energy work. Everything that will occur above this area and the witness will be a reality for the individual, no matter the distance. This is obviously very useful.

When you perform these exercises for the first time as part of your training, it is good to work with a partner or a friend. Compare your observations at a distance with a direct examination. Later, you can use just the observation at a distance.

ANALYSIS OF THE AURA AT A DISTANCE

As strange as it may sound, it is possible to read the aura at a distance. To do so, you can use two techniques you already experimented with. The first is the use of your inner vision, and the second is radiesthesia. Both techniques will use the decagon and the witness. For advanced practitioners, it is possible to only use the witness. In one very specific situation, I didn't even use a witness—but such conditions are rare and require a very difficult mental and astral process.

EXERCISE 36: USING RADIESTHESIA

Before you start this examination, you must prepare your workspace. It's best to have a table and a chair facing east. On this table, place a beeswax candle, a decagon, the witness, your pendulum, any chart that could be useful for this examination, and your notebook.

1. Relax and observe your breathing.
2. For a few minutes, place your left hand on the witness, touching it with your fingertips. Hold your pendulum in your right hand.

3. Close your eyes and say the full name of the individual out loud, as well as your intention.

4. Activate your third eye as you have done in previous exercises. Raise your level of consciousness to the plane you want to observe. If you want to do an aura reading, you should be fully aware of your own astral aura. At this moment, the physical place—your table, the candle, etc.—is vanishing. It is becoming transparent, losing its physical reality. As you move your consciousness on the astral plane by raising your perception, the physical world fades, losing its density. A real superimposition of planes allows you to connect with the subtle bodies of the witness and the subject of your research. Then, visualize the presence of the individual in front of you.

5. Continue to be fully aware of this astral connection and proceed to the aura reading in the same way you did in Exercises 22 and 24. You can keep your left hand on the witness, or you can remove it if you don't need it to maintain contact.

6. When your observation is complete, replace the pendulum, remove your hand from the witness, and come back to your own astral body. Take the time to feel your aura and its limits, colors, and vibrations. Then, progressively come back to your physical body and to the movement of your chest.

7. Open your eyes and record your observations in your notebook.

EXERCISE 37: VISUAL EXAMINATION OF THE SUBTLE BODIES

In the previous exercise, you used radiesthesia to observe the aura of the individual. Here you will use your astral vision to achieve the same goal without using any tools such as a pendulum. It is a good idea to work with a partner for this exercise.

FIRST EXPERIMENT

For your first experiment, we suggest observing the etheric body. Remember that this subtle body is the direct manifestation of the general health of an individual. Therefore, it is easy to receive feedback from your partner about your observations.

1. Have a discussion with your partner and choose a week the two of you will work together at a distance. For one week, each of you should take daily notes about your energy: fatigue, stress, overall health, etc. Everything relevant to your energy should be recorded.

2. At least five days out of seven, each individual should practice the visual examination of the etheric body of their partner. Don't tell your partner the days and times you are practicing this examination. When you see your partner's etheric, record every detail, along with the day and time of your observation.

3. At the end of the week, meet and compare your notes. This is an advanced exercise, but it is very useful. You can learn a lot, and this is the only way to progress.

SECOND EXPERIMENT

The second experiment is performed in exactly the same way—the only difference is the level of your aura reading. This experiment uses the astral aura.

1. Have a discussion with your partner and choose a week the two of you will work together at a distance. For one week, each of you should take daily notes about your mood and the emotions you feel throughout the day. Everything relevant to your mood should be recorded.

2. For at least five days out of seven, each individual should practice the visual examination of the astral aura of their partner. Don't tell your partner the days and times you are practicing this examination. When you see your partner's astral aura, record the colors, the way the energy flows, and anything unusual. Try to distinguish between colors that are parts of the underlying tendencies and temporary ones.

3. At the end of the week, meet with your partner and share your notes.

EXERCISE 38: ACTION AT A DISTANCE

As we've said several times, seeing the subtle bodies is great, but it is not enough. You should be able to act, if necessary, for the good of the individual you're observing.

1. Proceed in the same way as you did in exercise 36, with a witness. When contact has been established with the aura of your partner, you can transition to the action itself.

2. Place your hands in front of you, palms facing each other. Your hands should be eight inches (twenty centimeters) apart. Visualize a green sphere with sparkles of gold. Increase the density of the color while breathing.

3. When the sensation of the sphere is clear, move both hands in a single movement in the direction of your partner. At the same time, visualize the sphere going into your partner's aura. Keep it in your mind for few seconds with the intention of bringing energy and health.

4. Release your visualization and come back to your breathing.

5. End the exercise in the usual manner and record any details, including the time you took the action.

This is a very simple action that is very effective. There are a lot of possibilities when using the sphere technique. We recommended using the colors green and gold because they increase the energy and health of your partner. You can also experiment with the color vermillion if you feel your partner needs more energy, but be careful about the kind of red you choose. See chapter 9 to avoid any mistakes.

Chapter Thirteen
THE OUT-OF-BODY EXPERIENCE AND THE AURA

The out-of-body experience is a topic directly related to the aura and subtle bodies. The idea is that one of our subtle bodies can move away without cutting the link with the physical body. Our consciousness could move with it—or not. If it does, then you can be aware of a different location, a spiritual realm where you are not there physically, but "in spirit."

To understand how this phenomenon occurs, we must consider the difference between auras and subtle bodies. We have used these two words in this book in a similar way. We have defined the aura as an energy field surrounding the body, often as flows or radiations. Each energy field is related to a specific plane. The physical realm is closer to the etheric, and the causal body is more subtle. We also described the process that took place during embodiment of the soul and the way the auras were developed. Each aura is linked to a specific body. For example, the etheric is the energy field of the physical body. It is easy to observe the etheric, but this is not the case for the other subtle bodies. As a matter of fact, the higher we consider the subtle planes, the less the body and its aura can be distinguished. Thus, the astral body and the astral aura can easily be considered separately. This is not the case for the mental body and the mental aura, as they are closely combined.

In the first chapter of this book, we explained that everything in the world is energy. Visible matter is made of emptiness, but the frequency of vibrations of atoms makes them visible to our eyes. In some of this book's exercises, you changed your vision to see a larger spectrum than expected and even used psychic abilities to see the other plane. The difference between the astral aura and the astral body is a matter of density.

In the physical world, we used to consider that we cannot be in two different places at the same time. The exercises in this book have demonstrated that this may be true on the physical plane, but not on the other planes. In fact, quantum physics has recently demonstrated that a particle can be in two different places at the same time.[16] Ancient traditions say the same thing for subtle bodies and our consciousness. The thing is, these traditions taught techniques that allowed people to experiment with this phenomenon. That is what we are trying to provide in this book.

People have a natural tendency to believe that nothing is leaving our body, that there is no such thing as an aura. This is because feeling like our being is complete is essential for us. Many of us fear feeling detached from the world around us; this fear could also extend to out-of-body experiences. Instinctively, because we are doing everything we can to maintain the integrity of our being, we have doubt about experiences like exploring the aura. Doubt is needed to keep our inner stability. At the same time, everyone should open their minds to the possibility of exteriorization of subtle bodies.

Some natural phenomena allow the astral body to leave the body. This can happen during sleep. Dreams can be the result of such out-of-body experiences. Consequently, it is not surprising to learn that the Western tradition compares sleep to a small death. This idea comes from the belief that the soul represented by the astral body leaves the physical vehicle to travel in the celestial world. Obviously, not all dreams are phenomena of this kind, but some of them certainly are. In this case, sensations and memories are remembered differently. When we wake up, the dreams seem more vivid and not strictly belonging to our unconscious. We spontaneously feel that something different happened.

---

16. Letzter, "Giant Molecules Exist in Two Places at Once."

However, sleep and dreams are usually an involuntary process. The out-of-body phenomenon is spontaneous and the memories we bring back from this travel are usually distorted. This distortion is due to the absence of specific practices intended to voluntarily transfer our consciousness into the astral body. As the process was spontaneous, we were not able to receive and memorize in a proper way. In the same way that we have been able to learn to see the aura, there are techniques that allow us to separate full awareness in our astral body from the physical body. But we are never really separated from the physical body; we are always attached to it through a kind of umbilical cord of energy.

This cord is made from the same energy as the etheric body. Its color is usually identical to the etheric, but denser. It stays the same diameter all along, no matter how far the astral body travels. Like an umbilical cord, it maintains contact with the physical body. A close examination of this cord shows various flows of energy circulating. This movement of energy is like radio waves, a manifestation of the circulation of information and emotion. The astral cord is formed as soon as a subtle body separates from the physical body, voluntarily or not. It takes on the density that corresponds to the moving body and can therefore vary in appearance. This cord is not cut until the moment of death; it cannot be cut during voluntary or involuntary astral travel.

As we just explained, the cord connects the physical body via the etheric to the astral body. This could mean that only the astral body can separate from the physical body and travel on this invisible plane; in that case, the etheric body, or the mental body, would not be able to travel in the same way. However, experience shows that the mental body can also be separated and have the same kind of out-of-body experience. We call this *projection of the mental body* instead of *astral travel*. The technique is different, as you do not lose the awareness of your physical body while you travel. We cannot talk about a "mental cord"; such links exist as the equivalent of the astral cord. However, its level of vibration is so high that it is brighter and almost impossible to see. This kind of projection doesn't interrupt the normal activities of the body.

Under special circumstances, the etheric can separate from the body. It is comparable to the shift we observe sometimes in the aura. Such separation is not advisable, which is why it is usually unintentional. As the etheric body maintains the integrity and energy of the physical body, removing a large part of it slows down organic functions, weakens the body, and can lead to fainting. Fortunately, this process is very rare. There are a few cases that illustrate what we just explained; here are two examples.

The first occurred in a Russian school in 1845.[17] Forty-two students and other board members witnessed these strange phenomena. It began when the school hired a new French teacher. She was thirty-two years old. A few weeks after she started teaching, students began telling strange stories about her. Some were saying that the teacher was in the library, while others reported seeing her climbing the stairs to their classroom.

At first, no one really paid much attention to these stories. But they began taking things seriously when several incidents couldn't be attributed to simple mistakes. One day the teacher was writing something on the blackboard in front of thirteen young girls. The students suddenly saw a vaporous substance almost identical to their teacher leaving her body. The two shapes were standing side by side. One was writing on the board and the other one was doing the same movements, but without any chalk. After a close interrogation of the students, the facts were confirmed, but the staff decided to maintain the teacher's position.

This kind of phenomena continued to occur over the following weeks with more sightings. One day students saw the ghostly figure of their teacher in the refectory imitating the movements of the physical body seated a few feet away. Another time, students saw the ghostly figure walking in the classroom, although the teacher was sick and confined to her bed. One of the most significant episodes reported occurred when forty-two girls were doing embroidery. Through opened glass doors, they could see the whole garden. A few steps away from the building, their French teacher was picking flowers. A few moments later, the professor in charge of supervising the students left the room. The young girls then saw, with amazement, their French teacher sitting in the professor's chair! She was silent and motionless. A quick glance in the garden was enough to convince them that their French teacher was

---

17. See Flammarion, *La Mort et son Mystère*, and Aksakof, *Animisme et Spiritisme*.

still picking flowers. However, she was moving very slowly, as if she had no strength anymore or was asleep on her feet.

Getting used to the bizarre phenomena, two of the students stood up and tried touching the ghostly figure. They later stated that they felt a slight resistance comparable to that of a very light fabric, like muslin. The student who was standing slightly closer to the figure said that she passed her hand through the figure without difficulty. Oddly enough, the ghost didn't seem to be bothered at all by the actions of the two students. It remained visible for a few moments longer, then disappeared. At that moment, the movements of their teacher, who was still in the garden, returned to normal. When the French teacher was told what had happened and asked about her sensations during that time, she replied that she had seen her colleague come out to the garden and had thought that the students would surely be agitated.

For a year and a half, students and staff regularly witnessed such phenomena. Eventually, due to these incidents, the school had to ask the teacher to leave her position.

We could perform an extensive analysis of this amazing case, but it is not necessary. What is important is that this example clearly illustrates the separation of the etheric body of the teacher. Two observations are very significant: the physical body slowed down its movements during this phenomenon, and students felt pressure when crossing the ghostly figure. In this story, what was happening was involuntary and uncontrollable.

But we know that such phenomenon can be voluntary. This is what is used in spiritism when a medium expels a ghostly substance called *ectoplasm*. This kind of practice has been falsified countless times for various reasons. However, there are several cases that have been very well documented and demonstrate the reality of the etheric energy separated from the body. Separation of part of the etheric produces a significant weakening of the vitality of the subject. Such manifestation of the etheric is interesting because it gives a real demonstration of the existence of invisible bodies. I personally had the opportunity to directly experience similar phenomena.

In the 1970s, I was practicing and teaching hypnotism. This is a technique using suggestions to create a state of consciousness close to a deep relaxation. In this condition, the subject follows the words of the hypnotist, his will being deactivated by the suggestions. You can compare this state to your dreaming cycle during the night. The subject keeps a connection with the hypnotist he continues to hear; he can also answer the hypnotist's questions. At the time, I was exploring the use of hypnotism in out-of-body experiences. I was working with someone very receptive to hypnotism. One day I decided to experiment with the separation of the lower part of the subtle bodies, the etheric. It is important to note that the subject did not know anything about what I had planned.

The subject was lying on a sofa on one side of the room. Once in a deep state of hypnotic sleep, I asked him to move his consciousness to his etheric body. Then I asked him to imagine that he was moving in this invisible body to the other side of the room and to take the same position as the physical body. A few moments later, without saying anything, I took a needle and pricked where his etheric arm was supposed to be. Remember that, physically, he was on the other side of the room. In the material world, I was pricking an empty space. However, at the exact moment I pricked the empty space with the needle, he physically reacted with a moan as if he was feeling exactly what I was doing. After a few seconds, a small red mark appeared on his physical body exactly at the point I was pricking in the air on the other side of the room.

As you can imagine, it was a very strong and emotional experience. Even understanding the phenomenon, it was the first time I saw such a clear effect highlighting the link between the etheric and the physical bodies. For this reason, any out-of-body experience should be performed very carefully. It is very important to project the highest level of subtle bodies to avoid any such effects. As we saw in the first story and in my personal experience, not doing that could be very dangerous.

Finally, I want to emphasize the fact that astral travels are happening on the astral plane, which is linked to emotion, but also illusion. It is the place in which mental representations of our desires can take shape. Consequently, authentic experiences of astral travel can potentially lead to delusion. The astral world the subtle body travels in may confuse our mind. Our unconscious can generate false images of masters, locations, and actions that could merely be a representation of our desires and hopes. The same thing can occur for memories of past lives or old memories from this life.

I am not saying that everything on the astral plane is false, but rather that a shift in our perception of reality can deceive us with visions and sensations that seem true. To avoid such situations, it is important to limit the number and duration of our experiments. Before performing anything related to out-of-body experiences, it is important to practice and master the vision of the aura. It is a real foundation that helps you avoid illusion and get used to these perceptions.

Chapter Fourteen
BENEFITS OF AURA WORK

It all started with curiosity and desire. You have walked on a path as old as humanity.

Something buried deep within you has been felt, and you have asked yourself one of the most essential questions: *Who am I?* That question is what drove you to this book and this amazing journey. Platonic philosophy teaches that you came into this life with a memory of the spiritual world and your past lives. This essential part of who you are has always been there, waiting in the darkness of your unconscious. And it was not totally silent—you felt a desire for something higher, for a knowledge that was lost. You have always known that coming back to the real world, to the blissful world, required a unique thing, at the same time simple and extremely complicated: to "know thyself." As stated by the tradition: "Know thyself, and thou shalt know the Universe and the gods." From the knowledge of yourself, you will rise to the immortal divinities and the cosmos, leading you to the divine world your soul belongs to.

This study of yourself can be achieved in various ways. Each of us is moved by different memories and desires. We could be driven to learn about biology, anatomy, medicine, physics, or mathematics, to say the least. Or we could be driven by a strong desire to discover our occult anatomy. This is what you did in this book, and we are now walking together on this fascinating path.

As the Socratic principle states, "The only true wisdom is in knowing you know nothing." This understanding is the best support for this kind of training. We may be tempted to act as though we know better than others; as our psychic abilities develop, we could manifest a strong pride, maybe even a state of egocentricity. The remedy is humility. A lack of humility will lead to a state of delusion where reality will vanish and we will become forever haunted by the ghosts of our vanity. This is the major obstacle we must avoid, knowing that it will present itself over and over again throughout our journey.

AWARENESS

The first step was a call. You heard it and followed genuine intuition. You started to bring light to the darkness of your sensations. To go further, opening your eyes was essential. You had to find your real vision, which is forgotten during our embodiment. Each exercise in this book was intended to help you recover this ability. Enhancing your physical vision gave you the power to cross the threshold of this ghostly world. Lights of the etheric were revealed to you and you felt, maybe for the first time, that the world we live in is just a facade. This awareness is essential—from this awareness, your inner vision can be reactivated. Your third eye started to blink, seeing for the first time the shining lights of your aura. Your emotions became visible, and what was once a comforting theory became a reality. Around you, the beautiful flow of energy demonstrated your connection with the cosmos. These colors revealed a real expression of who you are at this moment of your life. You realized that there are other planes of reality. You crossed the emptiness to witness the manifestation of the archetypes.

Being aware of these emanations gives you the freedom to choose the spiritual world you want to live in. Few have reached this understanding, and even fewer have chosen. Everything starts with simple steps and exercises. The awareness of these subtle bodies changes one's reality. It gives you access to the real knowledge that only comes by doing and living. This inner vision has extended your awareness to the perception of the soul itself. This is the highest state you can reach using your psychic abilities. It is the inflection point when your entire life can become different forever. Again, here, pride and delusion are waiting for you. Your new awareness of the aura, its centers of energy, and its colors helps you repel these maleficent ghosts.

MASTERY

It is quite easy to read a book, memorize a set of unverified theories, and then pretend to know everything. You could spend your time convincing yourself that the work is done. But nothing is really achieved without mastery. Everything you learn, everything you practice, is a double-edged sword. Your knowledge gives you power. Your training strengthens your psychic abilities and increases your effectiveness. This is the first step toward mastery—if you know a secret and decide to apply it. Mastering these abilities, this vision, this power, means having strict morals and learning how to balance your spiritual and material life.

These abilities are a great thing, but they can become a dangerous tool, especially when used on others. Even the best intentions can lead to mistakes. Never forget that you are a human who can fail or be deceived. As such, everything you say during an aura reading must respect the freedom of the one you are observing. Your words must be open and constructive. Everything must be the description of a state that can evolve. When applied to yourself, you must always keep your perceptions under control.

Mastering your powers means you should not use them all the time. Your soul descended into a physical body for a reason. You cannot ignore this fact, and everything you do should be an expression of the right balance between the spiritual world and the material world. Mastery is reached when you can use your new abilities whenever you want, stopping them to enjoy your material life.

CREATION OF THE SOUL

You have heard the echo of this inner voice, and you have felt the presence of a divine part within you that we can symbolically compare to divine gems. At the end of this training, it is time to go forward and focus on the essential part of yourself. Your practice opened inner invisible doors that can unveil the mysteries of your soul. Your state of consciousness has changed. Now you can think about yourself in a more substantial way. Who are you and what makes you unique? How will your new abilities help you on this eternal quest of knowing thyself?

IMMORTALITY

This book was intended to answer your curiosity and give you the tools to start your inner journey. Know thyself and choose who you want to be!

Find the best personal way to balance body, soul, and spirit!

Practice empathy and unveil the treasures still hidden in your heart!

Raise your inner vision and focus on the higher subtle bodies!

Eventually, you will be powerful enough to cross the final threshold in full awareness, just as a rainbow of light shines before vanishing.

RECOMMENDED RESOURCES

- Online store and publications of Theurgia: www.theurgia.us
- Mediterranean yoga and Aurum Solis: www.mediterraneanyoga.org, www.aurumsolis.org
- Kabbalistic Order of the Rose-Cross: www.okrc.org
- Jean-Louis de Biasi websites: www.debiasi.org and www.facebook.com /jeanlouis.debiasi

I invite you to my Facebook page and my website, www.debiasi.org. I regularly post information about the workshops I offer, original blogs, and documents on topics related to this book. Charts that can be useful in aura readings can be found on my website as well. I also share updates from other websites.

BIBLIOGRAPHY

Aksakof, Alexandre. *Animisme et spiritisme: Essai d'un examen critique des phénomènes médiumniques.* Paris: Librairie des Sciences Psychiques, 1906.

Baraduc, H. *La force vitale: Notre corps vital fluidique, sa formule biométrique* [The vital power]. Paris, 1893.

———. *L'Âme humaine: Ses mouvements, ses lumières, et l'iconographie de l'invisible fluidique* [The human soul: Its movements, its lights, and the iconography of the fluidic invisible]. Paris, 1897.

Barton, Winifred G. *The Human Aura.* Québec, Canada: Éditions de Mortagne, 1971.

Becker, Robert, and Gary Selden. *The Body Electric: Electromagnetism and the Foundation of Life.* New York: William Morrow, 1985.

Besant, Annie. *Man and His Bodies.* London: Theosophical Publishing Society, 1896.

———. *The Seven Principles of Man.* London: Theosophical Publishing Society, 1892.

Cox, Simon Paul. "A Genealogy of the Subtle Body." PhD diss., Rice University, 2019. https://hdl.handle.net/1911/107458.

de Biasi, Jean-Louis. *Rediscover the Magick of the Gods and Goddesses: Revealing the Mysteries of Theurgy.* Woodbury, MN: Llewellyn Publications, 2014.

de Biasi, Jean-Louis, and Patricia Bourin. *The Ultimate Pagan Almanac 2019*. Las Vegas: Theurgia Publications, 2018.

Flammarion, Camille. *La mort et son mystère: Autour de la mort*. Paris: Ernest Flammarion, 1921.

Govinda, Lama Anagarika. *Foundations of Tibetan Mysticism*. York Beach, ME: Red Wheel/Weiser, 1969.

"History." Bio-Well. Accessed June 13, 2022. http://www.wwwl.bio-well.com /gb/history.html.

Iovine, John. *Kirlian Photography: A Hands-On Guide*. New York: McGraw-Hill, 1993.

Krippner, Stanley, and Daniel Rubin, eds. *Galaxies of Life: The Human Aura in Acupuncture and Photography*. New York: Gordon and Breach, 1973.

Leadbeater, Charles Webster. *The Chakras: A Monograph*. Wheaton, IL: Theosophical Publishing House, 1927.

———. *Clairvoyance*. London, 1899.

———. *Man Visible and Invisible*. London: Theosophical Publishing Society, 1902.

Letzter, Rafi. "Giant Molecules Exist in Two Places at Once in Unprecedented Quantum Experiment." *Scientific American*, October 8, 2019. https://www.scientificamerican.com/article/giant-molecules-exist -in-two-places-at-once-in-unprecedented-quantum-experiment/.

Mead, G. R. S. *The Doctrine of the Subtle Body in Western Tradition*. London: Theosophical Publishing House, 1919.

Ostrander, Sheila, and Lynn Schroeder. *Psi: Discoveries Behind the Iron Curtain*. Englewood Cliffs, NJ: Prentice-Hall, 1970.

Plutarch. *The Parallel Lives*. London: Heinemann, 1919. https://penelope .uchicago.edu/Thayer/E/Roman/Texts/Plutarch/Lives/Alexander*/9 .html.

Ratcliffe, Susan, ed. *Oxford Essential Quotations*. 5th ed. Oxford: Oxford University Press, 2017. https://www.oxfordreference.com/view/10.1093/acref/9780191843730.001.0001/q-oro-ed5-00004202.

Satchidananda, Sri Swami. *The Living Gita: The Complete Bhagavad Gita*. Yogaville, VA: Integral Yoga Publications, 1988.

Turner, Christopher. "Mesmeromania, or, the Tale of the Tub." *Cabinet* 21 (Spring 2006). https://www.cabinetmagazine.org/issues/21/turner.php.

INDEX

TO WRITE TO THE AUTHORS

If you wish to contact the authors or would like more information about this book, please write to the authors in care of Llewellyn Worldwide Ltd. and we will forward your request. Both the authors and publisher appreciate hearing from you and learning of your enjoyment of this book and how it has helped you. Llewellyn Worldwide Ltd. cannot guarantee that every letter written to the authors can be answered, but all will be forwarded. Please write to:

Jean-Louis de Biasi
Patricia Bourin
⅏ Llewellyn Worldwide
2143 Wooddale Drive
Woodbury, MN 55125-2989

Please enclose a self-addressed stamped envelope for reply,
or $1.00 to cover costs. If outside the U.S.A., enclose
an international postal reply coupon.

Many of Llewellyn's authors have websites with additional information and resources. For more information, please visit our website at http://www.llewellyn.com.